EV

TO GOD IN PRAYER

A Writer's Weekly Devotional

Kelly Boyer Sagert

Loconeal Publishing

Amherst, OH

Everything to God in Prayer

Loconeal books may be ordered through booksellers or by contacting:
www.loconeal.com
216-772-8380

Loconeal Publishing can bring authors to your live event.
Contact Loconeal Publishing at 216-772-8380.

Published by Loconeal Publishing, LLC
Printed in the United States of America

First Loconeal Publishing edition: December 2015

Visit our website: www.loconeal.com

ISBN 978-1-940466-42-2 (Hardback)
ISBN 978-1-940466-48-4 (Paperback)

Testimonials

"Filled with anecdotes from her own faith journey in the midst of trials, *Everything to God in Prayer* by Kelly Boyer Sagert is a unique devotional for Christian writers. You will love Kelly's warm style, grace-filled prayers, and insightful exercises designed to recharge your motivation to write. I highly recommend it!"

> ~Jeanette Levellie, author of *Two Scoops of Grace with Chuckles on Top, The Heart of Humor,* and *Shock the Clock: Time Management Strategies for Writers*

"*Everything to God in Prayer* is a devotional book that will inspire you to a fresh understanding, a new beginning, and a positive outlook, through transformational prayer and Scripture application. Praying God's Word over our lives and circumstances illuminates our souls with God's presence, shining His Light in our darkest areas, coaxing and encouraging us to discard our old ways and follow Jesus wherever He may lead, a journey every believer travels for the sake of the Gospel."

> ~Linda Kozar, author of *Babes With A Beatitude: Devotions For Smart, Savvy Women of Faith* and the Christian cozy mystery series, *When the Fat Ladies Sing*

There is no better way I can think of to hold onto the fact that God is with us daily than for us to write it down. That is what really sets Kelly's devotional apart. This book not only offers us something to think deeply about. It helps us transform a thought into a writing endeavor. This simple action takes us past the limitations offered by a mere moment of contemplation. We are given the opportunity to write in ways we may never have encountered on our own. Kelly asks us brilliant and elegant questions as she prompts us to jot down the goodness of God. Trust me when I say this book will not only help us now, but in the decades to come."

~Daniel Vasi, author of *Christian Babe Alert* and *Tempted: Powerful Strategies to Fight Everyday Temptations One Battle at a Time*

Dedication

This book is dedicated, with love and gratitude, to the Smucker family: Reverend Jim, Sharon, Jason, Kirsten and Nathan. A small portion why is described in the devotional for week 44.

Contents

Forward 1

Introduction 3

Week 1 - Week 52 .... 7 - 115

Appendix I 119

Appendix II: Further Reading 121

Foreword

By Honorably Retired Reverend Louis A. Will

David, arguably Israel's greatest king, yet a flawed person like all of us, also had a creative side that cannot be understated. Somewhere in his journey to adulthood he learned how to play the harp. While it must have been a wonderful outlet for him throughout his life, it also brought joy and contentment to others. In addition, David, perhaps while strumming his harp in quiet moments, also used his creative juices to bring words to life and left to us some marvelous psalms, honest expressions of the range of human emotions, written in communion with God.

This is just one example of how much deeper each of us can go within ourselves using the arts to help us ease into those spaces not often found or even desired in today's world.

While the dictionary attempts to put a definition to "art," in reality it is a deeply personal and unanalyzable word. It is what each of us, if we allow it to happen, pursues and experiences in trying to find more meaning in our daily lives, and in our spirituality and our faith journey in service to the Lord.

Kelly Boyer Sagert, in this book of unique stories, Scripture verses, and optional exercises, invites the reader to be open to some suggested ways to begin (or even revisit) a journey on which we all travel, but may not really be focused upon. These weekly devotions, with some suggestions for practicing the theme of the week, are simply that—suggestions. Kelly encourages her readers to use their own creativity, too, in ways that will help bring art into their spirituality and, thus, deepen their fulfillment in ways that are uniquely theirs.

The reader will appreciate the honesty from Kelly, as she relates circumstances in her own life that prompted questions, but which also led to new and wonderful experiences in her own spiritual journey, part of which is shared in this series of weekly devotions.

As Kelly writes in her introduction:
"My hope for this book is that you use it to:
-Explore your spiritual life in more detail
-Define what ministries God has planned for you
-Create your own testimonies so that you can serve as a witness for Christ"

So, I invite you, the reader, to find a quiet place and time in which you can simply 'be.' Spend time with each week's devotional entry and theme. Then, with Kelly's words and suggestions as catalysts, visit your own 'artsy' side and experience ways to grow even closer to God. Your faith journey will truly be made more meaningful, and bring even more enhanced ability to be a loving ambassador for Christ!

Louis A. Will
Retired Clergy
Presbyterian Church (U.S.A.)

Introduction

I started writing this book during a tumultuous time in my life—and in the life of my church. I was once again an active elder in the Presbyterian Church, which meant that I was on the board of members who made key decisions for the congregation. During my first three years of service, the church suffered significant financial problems and went through multiple ministers. All was uncertain and, sometimes, even chaotic.

To add to the situation, in 2012, I was hospitalized with colon disease and underwent nine surgeries in just 14 months, four of them major and one of them an emergency. Right before my emergency surgery, I'd been told that, without a colostomy, I might not survive the night. With a colostomy, my bodily waste went into an external bag and it was a challenging way for to me to live during the eight months before the colostomy could be safely reversed. Plus, my work life was undergoing significant changes and I wasn't sure how that would affect my income—right when I had more expenses.

During this time, I found myself thinking, *Why me, God? Why does this all need to happen at once? Why now?*

Although I will never know all of these answers, at least not on this side of heaven, these years have been spiritually fruitful. I became the head of our church's spiritual life committee, a newly created one—where I invited members and friends to participate in a year of daily praying for our church. I've had the opportunity to write original prayers for our church's bulletins, newsletters and website, and more.

I helped to lead a committee to start an annual Christian writer's conference—the Northeast Ohio Christian Writer's Conference—and continue to serve on that committee. Plus, I started a monthly workshop at our church, free and open to the community, where we focus on spiritual writing so we can more confidently share our testimonies of what Jesus has done in our lives. This program is beginning to spread to other churches, as well. I also have been taking turns as leader of an online devotional group, and I preached multiple sermons and led worship services in our church when we were without any minister at all.

None of this is intended as self-praise. Instead, I'm suggesting a partial answer to my questions to God. I believe that he used this confusing and painful time of my life to draw me closer to him—and to engage in faith building with others.

During this time, I also began writing this book. Each weekly devotional (with a couple of exceptions!) contains relevant Bible verses, devotional text and questions for you to answer in writing. Before you write your responses, set aside a quiet period of time to pray (using the prayer included in a particular devotional or sharing what's uniquely in your heart). Be sure to include time to listen for God's response.

My hope for this book is that you use it to:

- Explore your spiritual life in more detail
- Define what ministries God has planned for you
- Create your own testimonies so that you can serve as a witness for Christ

You may also be able to use what you've written to submit articles and blog posts to Christian publications, sharing your message to others who need to hear them and be encouraged in their own faith journeys.

Two quick notes before I begin:

- There are numerous translations of the Bible and I've used a variety of them sourced from Bible concordances. If you prefer a certain translation, please read the corresponding verses each week from your own Bible.

- I was raised with traditional language that referred to God using male pronouns. I have kept that language for simplicity's sake in writing.

God bless each one of you! I'd love to hear where this book takes you in your unique faith journey. I can be reached at kbsagert@aol.com.

Week 1

Therefore, if anyone is in Christ, he is a new creation. Old things have disappeared, and—look!—all things have become new! (2 Corinthians 5:17*)*

When my father was in high school, he took an aptitude test and, to his great surprise, results indicated that he should become a funeral director. He and his classmates enjoyed a good laugh—and then he went on to earn a marketing degree and get married. Soon after he got married, though, he felt himself pulled in the direction of—you guessed it: mortuary school. He went on to become a funeral director, eventually owning his own business.

Fast forward to when I was in high school: I took an aptitude test and the recommendation was that I become a journalist. I'd never considered that as a career and I decided that writing for a living would feel too much like having daily homework assignments, post-school. So, I disregarded the recommendation, even when my father shared his regrets over not paying closer attention to his own aptitude test results. I instead earned a psychology degree. Then, eight years later, I felt a strong urge to write for a living—and, although it took me several years to actually begin writing as a full-time career, that's what I ultimately did.

My father and I each got second chances at selecting careers. Fortunately, the second time, we both got it right, choosing fulfilling vocations. My father has had the ability to counsel and minister to people at one of the most difficult times in their lives, while I'm able to help people through what I'm shared in my writing, through Christian writer's conferences that I've helped to coordinate and the like.

Whether you're starting this devotional book at the cusp of a new year—or if you're starting at another time—you're involved in a beginning, something new and fresh. Whenever you begin something anew, you have a chance to do things differently, to live in a more positive and healthy way. As brothers and sisters in Christ, each day is a new opportunity to live in faith and to share God's love, mercy, grace and forgiveness with people that we meet.

Writing exercise:

Free write your answers to the three questions listed below, feeling free to deviate from them to take you wherever God leads you.

1) In what ways will you recommit yourself to Christ and the Christian life?
2) In what ways will you use your writing to minister to other people?
3) How will these two efforts work together?

Prayer:

God, I thank you for giving me new life through your son, Jesus Christ. Thank you for giving me a fresh start. Today, I recommit my heart and soul to you, asking your forgiveness whenever I choose a path other than your own. I ask that you guide me in whatever new direction will allow me to serve you best. All praise to you, the God of second chances! Amen.

Week 2

When Jesus had been baptized, he immediately came up out of the water. Suddenly, the heavens opened up for him, and he saw the Spirit of God descending like a dove and coming to rest on him. Then a voice from heaven said, "This is my Son, whom I love. I am pleased with him!" (Matthew 3:16-17)

Baptisms are typically joyous occasions. An exception was when my nephew, Doug, needed to be baptized at the Catholic hospital where he was born, shortly after birth. He was being transferred to Rainbow Babies and Children's Hospital in Cleveland because he was unable to breathe on his own. In fact, my sister and her husband needed to quickly name their newborn so that the hurried baptism could take place.

Unfortunately, he got worse. In fact, his blood pressure shot up to dangerous levels, to the degree that doctors needed to give him a drug to paralyze him so that he didn't have a heart attack. He was given blood transfusions and later needed to be tested for AIDS (negative!)—and a medicine that he needed could cause brain damage.

Fortunately, after a month of potentially fatal health complications, Doug began breathing on his own and his other symptoms resolved themselves—and we had a baptism celebration in our church to honor his life (held with the baptism for our own son, Adam). It was a doubly joyous occasion, for more reasons than one—and we still laugh when we remember how we all left the church, each of us thinking that someone else was giving my mother a ride home. (And, yes. When she called us, someone went back to pick her up!)

Each time that someone is baptized, you have an opportunity to consider what baptism means to you and your own personal relationship with Jesus Christ. The most important baptism of all—the baptism of Jesus—is commemorated in January. Some religious traditions place the baptism on the day of Epiphany, which is January 6. Other Christian churches commemorate this event during the second week of January—but, in reality, this is something to be celebrated *every* day.

Writing exercise:

Free write answers to these questions and go where God leads you in your writing:

1) What promises did you make (or were made for you) during your own baptism or when a child of yours was baptized?
2) How are you living out those promises today?
3) What can you do to further live up to those promises?

Prayer:

God, thank you for the blessing of baptism, which welcomes us into the Christian life and into your family. Help me to remember the promises made during my own baptism and help me to know my purpose in life. Forgive me when I get derailed and keep my focus on what truly matters—our redeemed existence in Jesus Christ. You are the God of new life! Amen.

Week 3

Always be joyful. Continually be prayerful. In everything be thankful, because this is God's will for you in Christ Jesus. (1 Thessalonians 5:16-18)

Traditionally, the Week of Prayer for Christian Unity is celebrated between January 18th and 25th. During this week, congregations pray for Christian churches and people around the world, and ecumenical prayer services are often held.

But whether you are reading this devotional in January or July, as a writer, you have the ability and privilege to write prayers that others can use. Although there is no one "right" way to write or say a prayer, it can be helpful to remember the acronym ACTS. This means that prayers should, overall, contain elements of:

- Adoration: praise and worship for God, the God of creation, of new life, of second chances, of love, grace, mercy and forgiveness
- Confession: admitting your sins (which God knows about, anyhow), asking forgiveness and promising repentance (turning around your ways)
- Thanksgiving: thanking God for the many blessings in your life and in the world
- Supplication: prayers for other people, whether for healing or other type of help

Now, I have to admit that, in my personal prayers, I tend to use TCSA (which sure isn't an easy acronym to remember) but the idea is the same. One of my goals is to also spend more time listening for God's responses.

Prayer is a personal conversation that you can have with God, anytime and anywhere. What's important in prayer: a humble and sincere heart. Each time that you pray, it's an opportunity to become closer to God and to discover more about what God wants for you in your life and personal ministries.

We can learn much about how to pray—and how NOT to pray—by reading Luke, Chapter 18. In this chapter, Jesus compares the prayers of a Pharisee, a highly respected religious man of his time, with that of a despised tax collector. Jesus prefers the prayers of the tax collector, who admitted that he was a sinner in need of redemption, to those of the Pharisee, who felt that he was above sin and better than others around him.

Humility or self-righteous pride? What is your attitude while praying? Jesus teaches that we should choose humility every time.

Writing exercise:

1) How do you pray?
2) How can you make your prayer time a deeper part of your life?
3) What answers have you gotten to prayer? When has God answered you in a way you didn't expect? How did this take your life in an unexpected way?

Prayer:

God, teach me to pray—for Christian unity and more. Teach me to humbly pray the way that brings me closest to you and help me to listen to your responses. Forgive me for times when I do not bring my thoughts and feelings to you, when I am self-righteous or when I miss opportunities to pray for others. You are an awesome God, always ready and willing to welcome me back. Praise God! Amen.

Week 4

For I am convinced that neither death nor life, neither angels nor demons, neither the present nor the future, nor any powers, neither height nor depth, nor anything else in all creation, will be able to separate us from the love of God that is in Christ Jesus our Lord. (Romans 8:38-39)

In January 2013, I needed to have 18 inches of my colon removed. Although the surgery was unpleasant, I was assured that it was successful and that I'd soon be feeling much better. Unfortunately, that didn't happen. And, by the time the resulting complications were discovered—over the Fourth of July weekend—the surgeon told me that, without emergency surgery, I might not survive the night.

It was a holiday weekend, remember, so the surgery department was closed. As I was being wheeled into the operating room, the surgeon was flipping on light switches and the medical team was bustling about. My body was bloated with disease and all was uncertain.

I briefly closed my eyes and, although I could still hear what was going on, I felt instantly transported to a sunny beach, sitting crossed legged on warm sand under a bright blue sky. I could hear the waves lapping against the sand and I could smell the earthiness of the beach and the tang of the water. I felt myself scoop up two handfuls of sand and hold them up to the sky.

As the crystalized grains of sand slowly fell back down to the earth, I felt myself saying, "It's all in your hands, God." In my vision, I felt myself smiling and, although I never saw any image of God, I certainly felt the reassuring returning smile.

So, I was totally at peace going into my surgery, which was an amazing gift. The eternal truth that nothing can separate us from the love of God—well, at that moment, I could touch that truth, see it, hear it, taste it, smell it. It was that real and nothing has been the same, ever since.

Writing exercise:

1) What is your own conversion story or testimony to Christ?
2) What has your faith enabled you to do?
3) How can you share your written testimony?

As writers, we are blessed to have the power of sharing what we write with others, many of whom are strangers that we'll never meet in person. This week, ask God to lead you in writing down your own personal testimony of Jesus Christ. How can your share this written testimony? Can you submit it to a magazine? Put in on your personal blog?

Prayer:

God, thank you for allowing me to come to you in prayer. It is an honor and a privilege. Today I ask you to guide me as I share my own story of what faith in Jesus Christ has meant to me. Please give me the courage to write honestly and from the heart and forgive me when I miss opportunities to share with others. You are an awesome God! Amen.

Week 5

When the time came for their purification according to the Law of Moses, Joseph and Mary took Jesus up to Jerusalem to present him to the Lord, as it is written in the Law of the Lord, "Every firstborn son is to be designated as holy to the Lord." (Luke 2:22-23)

According to Luke, Mary and Joseph took Jesus to Jerusalem 40 days after his birth, according to the Law of Moses. There, they sacrificed a pair of doves and met Simeon, a devout man who'd been promised by the Holy Spirit that he would live long enough to see the Messiah.

When Jesus arrived at the temple, Simeon pronounced that this babe would enlighten pagans, but that Mary's heart would be pierced by an arrow—a prophecy of her son's crucifixion. The prophetess Anna was also in the temple; she never left its confines, instead worshipping, praying and fasting. When she saw Jesus, she praised him for his role in the redemption of Israel.

This scene was frequently included in religious art during the late Medieval and Renaissance periods, including Ambrogio Lorenzetti's painting, *Presentation of Jesus in the Temple*, from 1342. Unique features of this painting include the gorgeous church architecture, Gothic in nature, which would have been familiar to 14th-century people and provides an overall feeling of mystery and drama.

This painting is remarkably different from Giotto's rendering from around 1320, Rembrandt's version from 1631 or Simon Vouet's version from around 1640. Thanks to the miracles of the Internet, we can look at photos of each of these paintings, as well as other perspectives of this holy event.

Perhaps, as my family is, you're even more fortunate. We live near the Allen Art Museum, which is located in Oberlin, Ohio, and contains a number of awe-inspiring Renaissance-era religious paintings—rich in saturated color—and statues. We are also close to the Cleveland Art Museum. We visit them often and leave feeling inspired. What art museums are in your area?

Writing exercise:

If you can visit museums with religious art, whether modern or more ancient, I strongly recommend that you do so. If that isn't practical, then immerse yourself in quality art resources online or in books. Write about what you see—and also how it makes you feel. In what way does meditating on this art make you feel closer to God and to his plan for your life?

Prayer:

Thank you God for the artists in the world who can inspire us with their talent and for their ability to illuminate us, centuries after they've put down their brushes. Thank you for giving me the ability to see and appreciate the beauty in this world. Help me to use the gifts you have given me in a way that honors and glorifies you, and guide me so that my words can inspire others to seek you. Amen.

Week 6

There is a season for everything, and a time for every event under heaven: a time to be born, and a time to die, a time to plant, and a time to uproot what was planted; a time to kill, and a time to heal; a time to tear down, and a time to build up; a time to weep, and a time to laugh; a time to mourn, and a time to dance; a time to scatter stones, and a time to gather stones; a time to embrace, and a time to refrain from embracing. (Ecclesiastes 3: 1-5)

We live in Northeast Ohio, very near Lake Erie, where the winds that whip over the frozen water come straight from Canada. In other words, it can get quite cold—and when it is, I'm always eager for spring and summer. And, even though my father also loves those seasons, from the time I was young he would caution me to enjoy *all* the seasons of my life, including late winter. Good advice—both when speaking of weather and about the rest of life.

Here's the bottom line: I can get impatient to get to the "good stuff" in life, wanting to skip over the sorrowful times—and even the more mundane ones. I doubt I'm unusual in that, but the reality is that plenty can be learned from challenging times. I spent much of two years either in the hospital or dealing with colon issues that would soon land me in the hospital again.

What I learned during that difficult season of my life:

- My family, church family and friends love me, whether I have a colostomy or not.
- Nurses really are angels of mercy.
- I can slow down my busyness and the world won't stop (and many won't even notice).

- This old adage is true: you should work to live, not live to work.
- You can have contentment, even peace, during difficult times. Even joy.
- Most important of all, God is truly with us in the challenging seasons of our life—in fact, more than ever before.

Writing exercise:

We all face dark times. Red ink overflowing in the checkbook. The affair after he swore that he wouldn't succumb to temptation, ever again. A seriously ill child. For this week's assignment, spend extra time in prayer before tackling the tough subjects in your own life. How do they make you feel? How has God helped you through them? What can you share with others to help them on their own sometimes tumultuous journeys?

Prayer:

God, help me to appreciate all of the seasons of my life and to appreciate the lessons that each has to teach me. Help me to not try to rush through darker times, through my weakest times because—when I am weak, you are strong. Forgive me when I rush through times of learning, when I doubt your presence in those times. Help me to praise you in all circumstances. Amen.

Week 7

Love is patient, love is kind. It does not envy, it does not boast, it is not proud. It does not dishonor others, it is not self-seeking, it is not easily angered, it keeps no record of wrongs. Love does not delight in evil but rejoices with the truth. It always protects, always trusts, always hopes, always perseveres. Love never fails. But where there are prophecies, they will cease; where there are tongues, they will be stilled; where there is knowledge, it will pass away. (I Corinthians 13:4-8)

I first met my friend, Debra Rose, after I wrote the script for my play, *Freedom's Light: A Stop Along the Underground Railroad*. She tried out and was awarded two roles. The first was that of an unnamed enslaved woman who came to a bitter end after being recaptured in her attempt to gain freedom. The second one was a savvy, courageous women who, after escaping slavery herself, became a conductor on the Underground Railroad, leading others to new life.

Debra is a talented actress, no doubt—and one powerful songstress! Her renditions of *Go Down, Moses*, *Wade in the Water*, *Follow the Drinking Gourd* and more gave me chills.

A couple of years after *Freedom's Light*, Debra and I collaborated on another venture, writing a play script about the Underground Railroad to be taken into elementary schools during Black History Month. At the end of one performance, Debra and I hugged, which startled one little boy into asking, "Are you friends?" When we said we were, he admitted that he didn't know that a black person and a white person *could* be friends.

Now, while it's easy for the two of us to love one another as sisters in Christ and as people who adore the arts, this boy was onto something important—that we often find it easier to love people who are "just like us," however that is defined. Jesus, though, gave us this commandment: "Love one another. As I have loved you, so you must love one another."

You notice that he didn't create any exceptions, any loopholes. So, that's one tall order!

Writing exercise:

Look in the news for a hot button issue where both sides may objectively have good points, but you have strong opinions on one particular side. This may be a political topic, a religious one—or whatever else is stirring up your emotions. Write a letter defending the *opposite* position as wholeheartedly as possible. Then free write about how you could love a person who embraces that side of the issue.

Prayer:

God—your love for me and for everyone is overwhelming. You sacrificed your only son for our sins and, through him, have given us eternal life. Help me to see everyone I meet as a child of yours— whether I agree with this person on issues of the day or not, whether he or she is "just like me" or not—and show me ways that I can express my love to others, now, tomorrow and always. Amen.

Week 8

So they nominated two men: Joseph called Barsabbas (also known as Justus) and Matthias. Then they prayed, "Lord, you know everyone's heart. Show us which of these two you have chosen to take over this apostolic ministry, which Judas left to go where he belongs." Then they cast lots, and the lot fell to Matthias; so he was added to the eleven apostles. (Acts 1:23-26)

One of the original twelve disciples, Judas Iscariot, betrayed Jesus for thirty pieces of silver—and, afterwards, hanged himself. That's a familiar story to churchgoers and Bible readers—but what isn't talked about as much is how the disciples handled the sudden gap in their small band of disciples. Can you imagine how they must have felt when one of their trusted band betrayed their master is such a brutal, bloodthirsty way?

They nevertheless resolved their loss in a practical manner. In these Bible verses, we see that they nominated two men and asked God to choose Judas's replacement—and it ended up being a man named Matthias.

This disciple was chosen after Jesus had ascended into heaven, but before the Holy Spirit had descended on the disciples on Pentecost. What's interesting is that the disciples didn't let the obvious sign of Judas's betrayal (only having eleven disciples) linger. Instead, they moved on with what mattered: spreading the Good News.

Betrayal is a harsh word, indicating something far more traumatic than a minor transgression against another and far more deliberate than an unintended act of harm. How do we move on from moments of betrayal?

Kelly Boyer Sagert

Writing exercise:

This is a four-part exercise. Because it may dredge up powerful emotions, pace yourself carefully and take breaks when needed.

1) Think back to a time when someone you trusted acted in a way that felt like betrayal to you. Although it's fine to write down what happened, focus more on how it made you feel and free write about that.
2) Think back to a time that someone else felt betrayed by you. How did this make you feel? Free write about that.
3) Remember a time that you didn't do as God would have wanted you to do—in other words, when you betrayed God's trust in you. Free write about how that makes you feel.
4) Meditate on God's all-encompassing forgiveness. How does that free you up to offer the same grace to another? What amends do you need to make? Free write about this entire exercise in a way that feels appropriate to you.

Prayer

God—we all hurt one another, in ways intended and unintended. Help me to forgive those who have sinned against me, to atone for times that I have hurt another and to confess my transgressions to you. Help me to pass on the grace that you freely grant me to others in my daily interactions with everyone I encounter. Amen.

Week 9

So they nominated two men: Joseph called Barsabbas (also known as Justus) and Matthias. Then they prayed, "Lord, you know everyone's heart. Show us which of these two you have chosen to take over this apostolic ministry, which Judas left to go where he belongs." Then they cast lots, and the lot fell to Matthias; so he was added to the eleven apostles. (Acts 1:23-26)

Yes. These are the exact same verses. Have you ever had a Bible story really stick with you—even though it's not one commonly focused upon? This is one of those for me, so please bear with me as I take this in a different direction from last week's devotional.

I've always been a fan of the underdog (and, as a lifelong fan of Cleveland sports, that has stood me in good stead). Heck, when I was a toddler, my favorite cartoon was titled *Underdog*. In this animated series, Underdog was the alter ego of the mild-mannered Shoeshine Boy who was able to eat a super energy pill, stored in his ring, to gain superpowers. He used them to protect the woman he loved, Sweet Polly Purebred, and he would say dashing things such as, "There's no need to fear, Underdog is here!"

It's not surprising, then, that I feel bad for Barsabbas. He apparently had been a follower of Jesus from the start. When Judas Iscariot was no longer living, having hanged himself after betraying Jesus, Barsabbas was one of the two leading candidates to replace him. However, the honor went to Matthias—and we don't really know what happened to Barsabbas.

According to *A Cloud of Witnesses, Saints and Martyrs from the Holy Land* by Bishop Demetri Khoury, Barsabbas became the Bishop of Eleutheropolis and was eventually martyred for his belief in Christ. Another tradition says that he drank from a cup of poison but wasn't harmed—and a book that did not become canonized, the Acts of Paul, recorded that Nero imprisoned Barsabbas but an appearance of the newly martyred Paul caused Nero to order his release.

Regardless of the accuracy of these oral traditions and written records, I have no doubt that God had a special plan for a man who was a believer from the start and who was faithful enough to be considered as a replacement for Judas.

Writing exercise:

Think of times when you have felt like the underdog. Did you want to get married, but always seem to be the bridesmaid (or groomsman)? Have you found yourself being the runner-up for coveted jobs? How does that make you feel? What plan do you think God has for your life? How do these experiences make you feel more compassion for people who are struggling?

Prayer:

God—you are all knowing and all wise. Forgive my doubts when I question the direction that you're taking my life. Help me to understand that you have masterfully created a unique plan for my life, unlike the one you have for any other human being, and guide me into fulfilling the special role that you have for me. Amen.

Week 10

"A new command I give you: Love one another. As I have loved you, so you must love one another. By this everyone will know that you are my disciples, if you love one another." (John 13:34-35).

I have a cousin, Ted, who is almost the exact same age as me. We had a fantastic time growing up, going on vacations together and otherwise just being cousins. One summer, when we were about ten, we were staying at a cottage at Chippewa Lake with our families—and, that summer, Ted desperately wanted to get a Johnny Bench baseball card. So, we'd head down to the corner store every morning to spend a nickel each in the hopes of getting this elusive card.

After a couple of weeks of disappointment, while opening up a pack of cards, Ted began pumping his fist in the air with celebration. "I got it," he shouted. "I got Johnny Bench!" After we hooted and hollered for a while, I said, "Boy, I wish I could get one of those." After looking somber for a moment, Ted silently handed me the card. "Here," he finally said. "You take it."

"Oh, no!" I told Ted. "This is yours. Why would you give it to me?"

"Because," he said, as if it was very obvious. "You want it—and I want *you* to be happy!"

Wow. Just . . . wow.

I didn't take the card, of course, but that story has stuck with me for a lifetime—mostly because of what Ted was willing to do for me, but also in part because he has Down's syndrome and is therefore allegedly not as smart as the average person. But, as the Day of Johnny Bench proved beyond any reasonable doubt, Ted actually has a much better sense of what truly *matters* than just about anyone else I know.

Sometimes, as Christians, we define the concept of "loving" as something huge and dramatic—which it can be. But, it can also be as simple as loving your new Johnny Bench card, but loving the other person more.

Writing exercise:

Cartoonist Scott Adams (*Dilbert*) has been quoted as saying that no act of kindness is small as each has a "ripple with no logical end." What acts of kindness have you been blessed with? Free write your answers—and then think about how you might perform your own acts of kindness this week. Where might these acts ripple? Don't be afraid to use your imagination! It's a gift from God.

Prayer:

God, please help me to love the people that I meet as simply and purely as Ted loves. Help me to realize that every day and every circumstance and situation offers an opportunity to offer up this love. Forgive me when I miss these opportunities and help me to see them in the future with clear eyes and an innocent heart. Amen.

Week 11

Therefore, as God's chosen ones, holy and loved, clothe yourselves with compassion, kindness, humility, meekness, and patience. Be tolerant of one another and forgive each other if anyone has a complaint against another. Just as the Lord has forgiven you, you also should forgive. (Colossians 3:12-13)

When my husband Don and I were newly married, we vacationed in South Carolina, stopping first at Charleston for a glimpse of history and then to Myrtle Beach to visit our cousins, Tom and Jo. While still in Charleston, we ate at an outdoor café. The weather was gorgeous and I felt relaxed and calm, at peace with the entire world.

Then, a woman walked up to us. "Y'all from the North?" she asked.

Startled (because we hadn't been talking, so our "accents" couldn't have given us away!), I said, "Yes. How did you know?"

She sat down next to me and started to ferociously drum her fingers on the table and tap her foot against the ground. "Because," she drawled, "y'all do THAT."

Here I was, more laidback than I'd been in a long time—and yet, she was right! I was tapping my fingers and foot as if I had somewhere very urgent to be—which is a pattern of mine. I may have all evening to go grocery shopping, let's say, and yet I race down the aisles as if in a stock car race. I've even been known to assign someone else every other aisle so that we can get the shopping done in half the time.

And, for what? Sometimes, of course, there is a good reason for faster movement. Perhaps I need to pick up someone who doesn't have a car or maybe I need to go to work. And yet, even when I have nowhere else to be, I'm *impatient*.

Take another look at this week's Bible verse. Yes, it talks about a whole lot more than just patience—but, if I don't cultivate the ability to pace myself, how could I possibly slow down enough to even *notice* that someone else needs to be treated with kindness and compassion? How do I bear with someone else if I don't give myself enough time to really listen what he or she is saying? What else am I missing out on by always being in a rush?

I now deliberately try to slow down enough to literally smell the roses, if I'm walking past a garden, or to notice bright green leaves in the spring—or how the ice sparkles on tree branches in the winter time. God has laid out all of this beauty for us, and slowing down enough to take notice is a form of thanksgiving.

Do it do it perfectly? Hah. It's a process.

Writing exercise:

What do you take for granted? What incredible things—or people—in your life go unnoticed because you're too used to being blessed by them? Free write the answer to those questions. And, if the writing contains people that you've taken for granted, write them a note to let them know how much you love and appreciate them.

Prayer:

God—help me to slow down to notice all of the beauty in the world and to hear you speaking to me. Help me to recognize who needs a listening ear or a touch on the shoulder. Guide me so that I can fall into the rhythm of life that you have planned for me and forgive me when I rush. I ask that you help me to live my life to the fullest, in just the way you have ordained. Amen.

Week 12

Then one of them said, "I will certainly return to you in about a year's time. By then, your wife Sarah will have borne a son." Now Sarah was listening at the tent entrance behind him. Abraham and Sarah were old—really old—and Sarah was beyond the age of childbearing. That's why Sarah laughed to herself, thinking, "After I'm so old and my husband is old, too, am I going to have sex?" (Genesis 18:10-12)

Emma Gatewood had lived an unremarkable life, earning an eighth grade education before becoming a farm wife. She and her husband had eleven children, and Emma worked hard to raise their children, plant crops, cook meals, create home remedies for illnesses and injuries and more. She had a tumultuous marriage and, after three decades, decided that she could not tolerate any more abuse, so she divorced.

When Emma was 67 years old, though, she did something incredible—she became the first woman to solo-hike the 2,000+-mile Appalachian Trail (AT), trudging up mountains and forging streams, sleeping and eating in the wild. She accomplished this after one failed attempt—at the relatively young age of . . . 66.

After that, she repeated her feat two more times, becoming the first person—man or woman—to solo-hike the Appalachian Trail three times. For an encore, she climbed the five highest peaks of the Adirondack Mountains and solo-hiked the Oregon Trail, beating the wagon that carried passengers by an entire week.

Let's face it. Emma Gatewood was darned OLD to be doing all of these things—just as Sarah and Abraham were when they gave birth to a child. Sarah laughed at the thought of becoming pregnant, just as Emma laughed at her first failed attempt to master the AT.

Here, I quote the play that I wrote about Emma, with Emma's words coming from a genuine diary entry:

"When she got into her room, she looked into the mirror and saw her reflection for the first time since she had started her hike. She saw a woman with broken, patched up glasses; a black eye that she had somehow sustained on the trail; and a sweater full of holes. She laughed at her appearance and, in her diary, wrote, 'I looked worse than a drunk out of the gutter. I had to laugh at myself.'"

What would you like to accomplish? Perhaps it's something that seems laughable, maybe because you think you're too old, or too weak, or too slow, or too tall or too short. Or whatever. The point is that, if you're doing God's will, none of that matters. Emma went on to be a founder of Ohio's Buckeye Trail, something that has provided exercise and enjoyment for countless people. God willed Sarah to become pregnant to begin a great nation, one that ultimately led to the birth of Jesus Christ.

What about you? What is God calling you to do today?

Writing exercise:

Answer that question: What is God calling you to do? If any of your answers seem outlandish, list why (I'm too young/I don't have the ability). Then, after each of those, answer yes or no to this question: if this is God's will for me, can God empower me to overcome this obstacle? At the end of the exercise, how are you feeling? Write that down, too!

Prayer:

God—you are all powerful and, through you, I can overcome all things. Help me to discern your plan for my life, to recognize the deepest desire that you have planted in my inner being. Forgive me when my faith is not strong enough to move the mountains that you created me to move—and give me the courage to pursue those dreams, listening all the while for your guidance. Amen.

Week 13

Clap your hands, all you peoples! Shout to God with a loud cry of joy! (Psalms 47:1)

Now may God, the source of hope, fill you with all joy and peace as you believe, so that you may overflow with hope by the power of the Holy Spirit. (Romans 15:13)

Picture walking into a sanctuary, where you're given a worship bulletin. Imagine your surprise when you're also given a brightly colored helium balloon and are told to release it when you feel joy during the service. How would you react?

Our minister, The Reverend Lou Will, told us that this happened in a cathedral-like Presbyterian Church in Scotland. There were no restrictions given. Perhaps you would feel joy simply by entering the sanctuary—or maybe a certain prayer or hymn would create in you a feeling of praise. The only guideline was that, when you felt joy, release the balloon.

Well, guess what? By the end of the service, about 1/4 to 1/3 of the people were still holding on to their balloons. Our minister speculated that some people might have felt silly releasing a balloon in church (after all, Presbyterians are among those known as God's "Frozen Chosen" for a reason), rather than assuming that a large percentage of worshipers had simply felt no joy during the service.

Meanwhile, I felt anxious throughout his sermon for an entirely different reason. I kept imagining that I had a helium balloon—and there were many times I felt joy—but I worried that, if I let go of my imaginary balloon too soon, then a better opportunity for balloon-releasing might occur, and I wouldn't have anything to release!

As you can see in the Bible verses chosen for this week's meditation, the Old Testament and New Testament alike encourage us in feeling joy. The psalm even tells us to express that joy through hand clapping and shouting—loud activities, indeed.

Meanwhile, the New Testament reminds us of the never-ending source of joy, the gift of the Holy Spirit. So, we never need to worry about running out of joy—which means whoever was blowing up the balloons of joy in that Scottish church would have true job security once we, as God's people, truly embraced this gift of the Holy Spirit.

Writing exercise:

What gives you great joy? Write down your feelings. If you could express them, knowing that nobody could see you, what would you do? Dance? Sing? Draw a picture using all the colors of the world? Write about that—as well as what is stopping you from living that life of joy, right here, right now.

Prayer:

God—I thank you for the gift of the Holy Spirit, the source of unending hope and joy. I ask that you fill me up with the Holy Spirit so that I can spread the message of your love, grace, mercy and forgiveness, far and wide—even further than the most helium-filled balloon in the universe. Use me, God, to spread the Good News of Jesus Christ, today, tomorrow—and for as long as I live. Amen.

Week 14

This is the day that the Lord has made; let's rejoice and be glad in it. (Psalm 118:24)

When my sister's best friend in elementary school, Karen, got a role in the school play, we were thrilled—even more so when we discovered that she had a speaking line! And, no. That was *not* a typo. Karen had *one* line. That didn't damper our excitement, though. We spent the next couple of weeks speaking her line in various ways (and using some pretty amateurish accents), emphasizing different words to see what worked best. Here are four examples:

- *I* can hardly wait for the weddin' (oooh . . . so who *wasn't* so thrilled about the big day?).
- I can hardly *wait* for the weddin' (hmmm . . . from whence comes the urgency?).
- I can hardly wait for *the* weddin' (oh, my! What makes *this* wedding so special?).
- I can hardly wait for the *weddin'* (ah! So you're excited about the wedding, but maybe not so much about the rest of the marriage? Tell us more!).

Unfortunately, I can't remember with certainty which version made it to the live performance (I'm thinking bullet point two?), but I definitely haven't forgotten the fun we had with our rehearsals.

Now, take a look at the Bible verse included for this week. Before I get out of bed each morning, I try to remember to say this verse. And, depending upon what I expect the day ahead of me to be like, I hear this verse in different ways. If I'm anticipating a good day, this verse is a joyful celebration of God's greatness.

Of course, not all days are likely to be good. After I had a series of colon surgeries in 2013 and 2014 (not all of which went according to plan!), I found myself dealing with plenty of free-floating anxiety. I would have nightmares where strangers would chase me with knives and all sorts of other unsettling scenarios.

On one of those types of mornings, this verse is more of a reminder to trust in God, that he'll get me through the day. Or, if I realize that I haven't been focusing enough on gratitude, this verse could be an admonishment to get my attitude and act together. Same words, different nuances.

Nevertheless, no matter what day it is: This is the day that the Lord has made; let's rejoice and be glad in it. Praise God!

Writing exercise:

Jot down some of your favorite lines, perhaps from your favorite book or the song that keeps running through your head. What are different ways that they could be interpreted, depending upon the current circumstances? What is it about that line that speaks to you? What message is it sending to you? How can you act upon its message?

Prayer:

God, I praise you for speaking to me in all circumstances, from the most joyful to those where I walk through the valley of the shadow of death. You always are with me and your peace and comfort always await those who seek you out. I ask that you help me keep a focus on you and to trust in your eternal love, no matter what my temporary situation may be. Amen.

Week 15

And when Jesus saw her, he called her to him, and said unto her, Woman, thou art loosed from thine infirmity. And he laid his hands on her: and immediately she was made straight, and glorified God. (Luke 13:12-13)

Although I've been using a variety of translations for this book of devotionals, often more contemporary ones, I needed for these two verses to be from King James. I do have a good reason!

A common thread in this book is how my life changed after a series of serious colon surgeries. In July 2013, I had an emergency colostomy, where the colon empties out of a hole in the abdomen into a bag. Although I'm grateful that this surgery was available, since my life was in danger, having a colostomy presents challenges that I'd never anticipated, and certainly not at my relatively young age. It took two attempts to reverse the colostomy and I feel very blessed to have had it successfully reversed.

The night I came from the hospital after my reversal, I decided to start reading a new book of devotionals from the large supply that I have gotten from library book sales. And, the one I picked up was by T.D. Jakes, titled *Woman, Thou Art Loosed.*

I can't fully explain the feeling that came over me when I read that title, after two long years of sickness, surgeries, pain and fear. What made these verses especially meaningful to me was that my colon had been made straight that day—and I was filled with feelings of praise.

Now, I don't know what the future holds (it's okay if you shout here, "But I do know who holds the future!"). I can say, though, that after that surgery, I have had at least a year and a half without any colon problems, any surgeries, or any hospitalizations. So, it's understandable that these verses are among my favorites.

If you read the rest of the story in Luke (verses 14-17), you'll see that Jesus healed this woman on the Sabbath, for which he received much criticism by the synagogue leader. But, the people who were following him were delighted. This tells me that I need to focus on loving others and on doing whatever good I can as a response of thanksgiving.

Writing exercise:

What about you? What Bible verses speak especially to you? Why? Free write your answers, not settling for the most obvious answers. You might be surprised!

Prayer:

God, I thank you for all of the ways in which you have blessed me— and continue to bless me. Help me to study your word and hear it afresh each time. You have a special plan for each one of us and I ask that you still our hearts so that we can hear the unique messages that you have for each one of us, your children. Amen.

Week 16

The Lord told Joshua, "Look! I have given Jericho over to your control, along with its kings and valiant soldiers. March around the city, all the soldiers circling the city once. Do this for six days, with seven priests carrying in front of the ark seven trumpets made from rams' horns. On the seventh day march around the city seven times while the priests blow their trumpets. When they sound a long blast with the ram's horn, as soon as you hear the sound of the trumpet, then the entire army is to cry out loud, the city wall will collapse, and then all of the soldiers are to charge straight ahead." (Joshua 6:2-5)

Now, why on earth would God tell Joshua's men to take such offbeat actions before he delivered the city to them? Literally—only God knows. This story reminds me of another war story, though, told to our family by a park ranger as we walked across Pickett's Charge in Gettysburg. (And, please note! This is in no way comparing Confederates with Nazis. My only intention is to illustrate the connectedness of life.)

He asked us to first think about the horrors of World War II, from concentration camps to war casualties, which conjured up ugly images beyond comprehension. He then asked us to consider how the Allied forces appreciated the United States when its military joined in the effort. By no means did the U.S. "win" the war, but they were certainly a welcomed addition to Allied forces.

Now, what if the U.S. hadn't been as strong as it was? That would be a factor in Adolf Hitler's favor, wouldn't it? And, let's face it, had the Confederates won the Civil War, the power of each country (the remaining "United" States and the Confederate States) would have been diluted.

Still with me? So, why didn't the Confederates win the war? They had early momentum. Well, the "high water mark"—meaning, the furthest the Confederates ever invaded the North—was in Gettysburg. And, the Confederates were doing pretty well in Gettysburg until the Union Army gained possession of Little Round Top, which was cleared-out high ground. After that, the momentum began shifting to the Union Army, with the Confederacy defeated less than two years later.

So, it could be said that the Nazis were ultimately defeated by the Union Army when they captured Little Round Top, more than 80 years earlier. Right?

Oh, and the ranger told us one more thing. Little Round Top had only been cleared of trees the year before, by the farmer who owned the property, because he needed the wood.

Now, is it possible that God had the farmer do this backbreaking menial work because he knew that the Nazis would need defeated? Who is to say, really? But this does tell us that God can use anything and anyone for good purpose, no matter how confounding it appears to human eyes.

Writing exercise:

What examples have you witnessed where God has used people in unexpected ways to achieve a good purpose? Also consider a current trouble in your life. How might God be using you? How can you see God turning your mess into a message, your test into a testimony?

Prayer:

God, your ways are not always clear. You have the perspective of eternity, while we can only understand life and its circumstances in a limited way. Help us to trust you in all circumstances and forgive us when we fall short. Help us to see your glory and purpose so that we can witness for you. Amen.

Week 17

Therefore we regard the message of the prophets as confirmed beyond doubt, and you will do well to pay attention to it, as to a lamp that is shining in a gloomy place, until the day dawns and the morning star rises in your hearts. (2 Peter 1:19)

I recently read *The Cloister Walk*, an amazing book by Kathleen Norris. The author shared how she, a lukewarm Presbyterian, became a Benedictine oblate. This book is part meditation, part memoir, part history and more, with its whole so much more than the sum of its parts.

And, when I read a phrase that Norris quoted from St. Gertrude, a mystical 13th-century Abbess, it hit me like a ton of bricks. The phrase is: *From all heedlessness in my behavior, deliver me, O Lord.*

I spent weeks—no, make that months—trying to determine why this resonated so strongly with me. I ultimately came up with this conclusion: I sometimes sleepwalk through life, even though God has given me so much to notice, appreciate, enjoy. I long to make a difference in other peoples' lives and to live a life of intention but, instead, I sometimes just buy a frozen dinner and take a nap.

I reached a deeper understanding of heedlessness by witnessing the opposite: when two poet friends, Steve and Theresa, posted on Facebook about the environmentally-friendlier car they bought and of the vegan dinner they prepared. These issues matter deeply to this couple—and they live out their values. And that, my friends, is a very worthy goal.

Ultimately, I wrote this prayer:

God—forgiveness my heedlessness . . . I ask, I accumulate, I want— and yet, I pass by so much that has already been so freely given to me.

I rush, I run, I plan—and then I miss out on what you wanted me to see, what you wanted me to know, what you wanted me to experience. Slow me down, God.

You give me a love of words, and yet I sometimes use them carelessly, not thinking of the impact they might have. I speak out of frustration, I speak in a hurry—and then I don't speak at all when my words might have made a difference.

I fill my time with noise when what I needed was quietness, when what I needed to do was to reflect, when what I needed to do was meditate on your words.

From all heedlessness in my behavior, deliver me, O Lord.

Now, normally I end one of these weekly devotions with a writing exercise and a prayer. This time, I just shared a prayer that I wrote and I invite you to think of an issue in your life that troubles you—and to write a prayer that addresses your deepest concerns. Then, be attentive to that issue, as a lamp shining in a dark place.

Week 18~Guest Post

"Amen, I say to you, if you have faith the size of a mustard seed, you will say to this mountain 'move from here to there' and it will move. Nothing will be impossible for you." (Matthew 17:20)

Vacations are funny things. You rest from your routine but exert yourself on a whole other level as you stretch to accommodate the unexpected that is the fodder of trips into the unknown.

Like Disney World.

A crazy compilation of work schedules, business travel, financial considerations, and the much grieved but inevitable beginning of the new school year charted my destiny. I was given four days to prepare our family for a three-week road trip and wild tour through the Magic Kingdom. I suspect that the Holy Spirit was chuckling as I grappled to regain control of my once orderly universe. It didn't happen, but when the opportunity to write this little devotion came (whilst sitting in the back seat of our car to comfort my bored ten year old), I knew it was a quest I must fulfill.

I am not into hype. Las Vegas does not interest me unless it comes with all expenses paid and a nanny to care for my kids. So I can't say that I had stars in my eyes about going to Disney World. I decided that I would go quietly because I love my kids and knew that, no matter what, they would have memories to carry into their fast approaching young adulthood.

Disney World is remarkable most of all because it exists!!

There, I said it. This place sprung from a crazy idea!

Come on! A whole kingdom built around one man's imagination and his peculiar obsession with a mouse? But it DOES exist and continues to thrive and get bigger every year. I was fascinated by the number of different languages and accents I heard as we waited for the next ride or ambled through gift shops ablaze with the ubiquitous mouse ears.

Walt Disney was a man who came from very humble means. His father struggled to provide for his family. When young Walt announced that he wanted to become an artist, his father scoffed at the idea. But Walt was undaunted and continued to seek out opportunities to explore his love for illustration and cartoon characters. Over the course of half a century, he was to see his fortunes rise and fall dramatically. He lost everything more than once. At one point, he was pushing himself and his team of illustrators so hard that he suffered a nervous breakdown. He regrouped after a long rest. While taking his girls out to play at a park, Walt had a thought: families needed a place to have fun and enjoy being together. The concept of Disney World was born!

There is no doubt that Walt Disney was an incredible visionary but this quality was not his most exceptional gift. His greatest gift was that of faith. Walt seemed to know in his innermost being that whatever he envisioned could and would take shape through hard work, perseverance, and faith in the beauty of the dream and its goodness. By both his actions and his beliefs, he spoke to the mountains of naysayers, financial struggles, unknown territory and self-doubt. They moved, and his legacy continues to spark imagination and belief in others. No matter what you might think about the company today, its founder proved the words of Jesus to be true: "If you have faith . . . NOTHING will be impossible for you."

Writing exercise:

I didn't write this devotional. It was written by Gwen Evans (thank you, Gwen!) and I included it to encourage each of you to reach out and network with other Christian writers. Attend Christian writer's conferences (http://writing.shawguides.com/Tag/Religion) or start a group for writers at your church or local Christian bookstore. You have so much to offer other writers—and they have so much to offer you!

Everything to God in Prayer

Prayer:

Lord, so many dreams of mine have been put on the shelf because of circumstances I never expected. I have all but given up on them. Send me the power of your Holy Spirit to infuse me with new hope that these dreams are your gift to me and that even now I can still realize them, for you are with me to move every obstacle and make a way for my dreams to come true. Reveal to me the next good step to bring your dream for me into reality, and give me the faith and courage to take that step. Amen.

Week 19

Lord, make me an instrument of your peace; where there is hatred, let me sow love; where there is injury, pardon; where there is doubt, faith; where there is despair, hope; where there is darkness, light; where there is sadness, joy, (Opening of the prayer of St. Francis of Assisi)

After I got the contract for *Everything to God in Prayer*, I knew that I needed to go on a retreat to center my thoughts. I ended up spending two days and one night with the Sisters of St. Francis in Sylvania, Ohio, surrounded by an 89-acre animal sanctuary, plus gorgeous prayer gardens and statutes. There was even a replica of the chapel that St. Francis used for worship and it was open for prayer from 9 a.m. to 5 p.m. The trip was worthwhile for this chapel alone.

When I arrived, I was given a tour of the buildings and grounds by Sister Helen, the hospitality sister, and I ate dinner with a group of friendly and welcoming sisters. I spent the evening focused on a Bible study and prayer journey found in *Soul Motive to Pray: A Personal Retreat* by Sharon Recher Hoover—and then went for another walk around the beautiful grounds. The weather was perfect: sunny with a gentle breeze.

The next day, I went on a mini-pilgrimage led by Sister Joan, where we could appreciate the marvelous artwork found in the Lady Queen of Peace chapel and throughout the buildings, which are adjacent to those of Lourdes University. The stained glass windows were brilliant with sun-kissed vibrancy. The lifelike statues were demonstrations of saints gone before us, and I longed to touch the smooth and glossy tile work. All of the artwork was visually stunning—and emotionally and spiritually moving. The original Mother Superior had earned her masters of art degree in art in 1902, I learned, a woman ahead of her time.

During the mini-pilgrimage, we stopped at key locations on the grounds and prayed together at each, reflecting on questions, such as: how we can affirm the goodness of others who are not like us—and, perhaps most compelling of all, to consider what untamed wolf lies within each of us, and what that means for what still lies ahead.

St. Francis, I learned, believed that an outer journey triggers an inner one—and that life is a journey of ongoing conversion. He also said that, as God's servants, we are "his minstrels whose task it is to light peoples' hearts and move them to joy." What a privilege!

Writing exercise:

Consider planning a spiritual retreat of your own, if possible at a place that takes you out of your comfort zone. Write up a plan. If it isn't possible to leave home or your city, create a spiritual retreat that you can embrace wherever you are, using resources such as *Soul Motive to Pray*.

Prayer:

This is the second half of St. Francis's prayer:

O Divine Master, grant that I may not so much seek to be consoled as to console; to be understood, as to understand; to be loved, as to love; for it is in giving that we receive, it is in pardoning that we are pardoned, and it is in dying that we are born to Eternal Life. Amen.

Week 20

Don't you know that you yourselves are God's temple and that God's Spirit dwells in your midst? (1 Corinthians 3:16)

Have you ever seen a matryoshka doll, also called a Russian nesting doll? This "doll" is actually a set of them, in which painted wooden carvings of decreasing size are put inside one another. The dolls will look identical, except for the size.

I often use these dolls when leading spiritual writing workshops. I find them helpful to use as an analogy—but please note that the analogy is mine, not something inherently associated with these nesting dolls. The largest doll, I'll say, represents our body, which is needed to write anything. How could we write without our hands or, as a more modern option, without voice recognition typing software? When we rely significantly on our bodies to write, though, and not go any deeper, the writing tends to be doodles or random lists that require little thought.

The second doll, from my perspective, represents our minds. So when we use both body and mind to write, we can create text of more depth, perhaps how-to articles or grocery lists that will gather together all you need for a week's worth of meals. To me, the third doll represents our hearts—and, when we write with body, mind and heart, we can produce poignant essays (think *Chicken Soup for the Soul*) and loving letters to family and friends.

The fourth doll, in my analogy, stands for our souls. When we write from this level, we are creating something unique and special because we are expressing our deepest selves. This is the level of authenticity that we try to reach in the spiritual writing workshops—and this is where I'd like to encourage you to journey.

The fifth—and smallest—doll in the set represents (to me) the

Holy Spirit, something that resides in each of us but is outside of our personal control. It's my belief that the Holy Spirit plays a role in bringing the right mix of people together for writing workshops, creating the appropriate combination for whatever ministering and spiritual journeying should take place.

Writing exercise:

Go deeper! This week, choose one of the topics from a previous devotional and practice freewriting without stopping for 10 to 15 minutes at a time. If you get to a point where you have nothing more to say, it's okay to write "I'm not sure what I want to say next but that's okay because . . ." and you'll probably find yourself getting back on track. And, there is no wrong answer here so, as long as you continue writing, you can't really go off track.

Prayer:

God—I ask that you bless my writing as I use it to build a stronger relationship with you and to uncover what you have created me to do. When I write from my most authentic self, I'm really discovering what I already really knew, something that you've placed within me, your child who is wonderfully and fearfully made. Guide me, God, to use my writing to live out my true purpose. Amen.

Week 21

For the next two weeks, we're going a different route. We're going explore how substances that we encounter every day are used symbolically in the Bible—and then delve into what they represent to you. This week, we're looking at rocks. Here are just some of the ways that rocks are used as symbols in the Bible.

Rocks symbolize God:

- *"The LORD lives! Praise be to my Rock! Exalted be my God, the Rock, my Savior! (2 Samuel 22:47)*

Rocks symbolize a place of refuge:

- *Each one will be like a shelter from the wind and a refuge from the storm, like streams of water in the desert and the shadow of a great rock in a thirsty land. (Isaiah 32:2)*

Rocks symbolize strength:

- *Turn your ear to me, come quickly to my rescue; be my rock of refuge, a strong fortress to save me. Since you are my rock and my fortress, for the sake of your name lead and guide me. (Psalm 31:2-3)*

Rocks are used as symbols in conjunction with water (with rocks being a barrier—although broken down—to life-sustaining water):

- *He split the rocks in the wilderness and gave them water as abundant as the seas; he brought streams out of a rocky crag and made water flow down like rivers. (Psalm 78:15-16)*

Rocks are heavy and laying them down can symbolize this concept:

- *"Come to me, all you who are weary and burdened, and I will give you rest. (Matthew 11:28)*

Writing exercise:

After you have read these verses, feel free to use a Biblical concordance to find other ways in which rocks are used as symbols. A concordance helps you locate where words and terms appear throughout Scripture. Online ones include:

- http://www.biblestudytools.com/concordances/
- https://www.biblegateway.com/
- http://biblehub.com/concordance/

Armed with this knowledge, collect some rocks. Hold a rock in your hand for a while, meditating on the Scripture that speaks most to you. Does the rock feel smooth? Sharp in places? Cool to the touch? Then, do something with your rock: perhaps laying it down at the foot of a cross or burying it in dirt like a seed or placing it in a bowl of water.

Write down what those actions mean to you.

Prayer:

God—you are my rock. You are my strength and my salvation. (Now, finish this prayer with what you've learned about what rocks symbolize to you, spiritually speaking.)

Week 22

You know what to do here! Verses that use water as a symbol include:

Water symbolizes troubled times

- *Therefore let all the faithful pray to you while you may be found; surely the rising of the mighty waters will not reach them. (Psalms 32:6)*

Water symbolizes salvation and eternal life

- *He said to me: "It is done. I am the Alpha and the Omega, the Beginning and the End. To the thirsty I will give water without cost from the spring of the water of life. (Revelation 21:6)*

- *Jesus answered her, "If you knew the gift of God and who it is that asks you for a drink, you would have asked him and he would have given you living water." "Sir," the woman said, "you have nothing to draw with and the well is deep. Where can you get this living water? Are you greater than our father Jacob, who gave us the well and drank from it himself, as did also his sons and his livestock?" Jesus answered, "Everyone who drinks this water will be thirsty again, but whoever drinks the water I give them will never thirst. Indeed, the water I give them will become in them a spring of water welling up to eternal life." (John 4:10-14)*

Water symbolizes spiritual cleansing

- *I will sprinkle clean water on you, and you will be clean; I will cleanse you from all your impurities and from all your idols. (Ezekiel 36:25)*

Water symbolizes the Holy Spirit

- *On the last and greatest day of the festival, Jesus stood and said in a loud voice, "Let anyone who is thirsty come to me and drink. Whoever believes in me, as Scripture has said, rivers of living water will flow from within them." By this he meant the Spirit, whom those who believed in him were later to receive. Up to that time the Spirit had not been given, since Jesus had not yet been glorified. (John 7:37-39)*

Writing exercise:

Physically do something with water while meditating on the Scripture with the deepest meaning for you. Pour the water in a clear bowl, water thirsty flowers, sprinkle drops on your arm. Take a long refreshing drink and notice how the water feels on your tongue. Then free write what this means to you.

Prayer:

God—I praise you for your willingness to wash me clean, to remove all of my impurities. (Now, finish this prayer with what you've learned about what water symbolizes to you, spiritually speaking.)

Week 23

"For we are the product of His hand, heaven's poetry etched on lives, created in the Anointed, Jesus, to accomplish the good works God arranged long ago." (Ephesians 2:10)

Shortly after my last colon surgery, I was lucky enough to take a creative writing class from Eva Shaw. She had me free write for ten minutes in the first person as if I was a color. Here's what I wrote:

I am strawberry sherbet pink, the color of the carpet Grandma chose after Grandpa died and she could finally throw out all of the dingy grays, grimy browns and muddy greens.

I am the tinge in a young woman's cheeks when she realizes that, yes, he really does care about her, after all. I am the color that is more modest than fire engine red, more even-tempered than Scarlett O'Hara—and yet I am more audacious than hushed Melanie, and too vibrant for funerals or Amish gatherings.

I am the hue of confidence but not of arrogance. I am the tint of healthy self-esteem but not of raging ego. I am the color of joy, but not mania. I am the shade of restraint but not limitation. I am the color of life well-chosen after years of ping-ponging between dusky shame and blood congealing into scabs.

I am the eau de fearlessness but not of recklessness. I am the color of pride but not a shade that condemns others or compares our songs. I am pink. Strawberry sherbet pink swirled with just a touch of cream, rich cream, luscious cream.

I am the healthy color of a baby's bottom after a warm bath, the color of a mother's nipples after breastfeeding. I am pink. I say it decisively—I am pink—without any need to shout over your colors.

I am pink. Strawberry sherbet pink. Lovely, illuminating, life-affirming pink. Praise God, praise God, praise God. I am finally truly pink.

Writing exercise:

This is a two-part exercise. First, I want you to free write as if you were a color, in first person, without thinking too much about what you're writing. Just let the words flow. Then, take another ten minutes and write about what that exercise tells you about God's specific purpose for your life.

Prayer:

God—You have created each of us in your image—and yet you have given us each different gifts and strengths, challenges and weaknesses. You have written a timeless poem for each of our lives, and I praise you and glorify you for the life that you have chosen for me. Help me use my gifts—and even my weaknesses—to witness for you. Amen.

Week 24

Place my yoke on you and learn from me, because I am gentle and humble, and you will find rest for your souls. (Matthew 11:29)

In this Bible verse, Jesus is talking about a spiritual rest, but our bodies also need physical rest. If we don't take care of ourselves, then we can't love and care for others as we are commanded to do.

And, the reality is that nobody needs to tell me twice to take a nap! I love afternoon naps, since that's the time of day when I'm at my lowest ebb. In fact, if I know that I have a significant writing project, I try to plan a nap before beginning, knowing that I'll feel more refreshed and do a better job.

I was sharing that practice with my spiritual director and she confessed that she's also a lover of naps—and she also shared a phrase that she uses: *naptio divina*. This is a play on words of the term *lectio divina*, a Latin term meaning "divine reading."

This process was described by a Carthusian monk named Guigo in the 12th century in his book, *The Ladder of Monks*. This idea was not new to Guigo, as he was expanding upon the 6th-century practice of St. Benedict, but Guigo belonged to a contemplative order and so *lectio divina* resonated with him.

In this spiritual practice, we read Scriptures in a way that invites in God's presence in the hope that we can discern what God wants to say to us. *Lectio divina* has four main phases:

- Lectio (reading): we read reflectively, allowing the passage to sink in
- Meditatio (reflection): we reflect upon the text
- Oratio (response): we speak to God through our hearts, not our minds

- Contemplatio (rest): we let go of all, including spiritual thoughts, resting in the word of God and listening for his voice

Writing exercise:

Perhaps you'd like to pray over the verse used in this week's devotionals or maybe you'd rather choose another. After choosing a short amount of Scripture, calm yourself and just breathe and be. Appreciate the silence. Read the text, slowly and with care. Take a look at smaller portions of the Scripture. In the Scripture above, perhaps the phrase "gentle and humble" allows you to hear God's voice. Or maybe it's "rest for your souls."

Put no pressure on yourself for results, as you are giving yourself up to God's timing. There is no other goal—and, in fact, there is no ending prayer for this devotional because this is a truly personal process. I once spent a couple of weeks where I centered myself this way, without anything "happening." Then, one evening, I simply asked God what he wanted from me and I "heard"—not as an actual voice, mind you—just one word: "reconciler." It was a profound experience and I pray the same for you. Amen.

Week 25

Because I was hungry, and you gave me something to eat. I was thirsty, and you gave me something to drink. I was a stranger, and you welcomed me. I was naked, and you clothed me. I was sick, and you took care of me. I was in prison, and you visited me. Then the righteous will say to him, 'Lord, when did we see you hungry and give you something to eat, or thirsty and give you something to drink? When did we see you as a stranger and welcome you, or see you naked and clothe you? When did we see you sick or in prison, and visit you?' The king will answer them, 'I tell all of you with certainty, since you did it for one of the least important of these brothers of mine, you did it for me.' (Matthew 25:35-40)

For 15 years, my sister Tracy volunteered daily for an elementary school where 96% of the children lived in households that were at or below the federal poverty line. For a family of four, that was less than $23,850. Tracy collaborated with a Catholic organization to help get these children coats and she always made sure that they had new pencils with erasers on important test days—along with treats on holiday.

She noticed, though, that some of the children still seemed ashamed as they entered and exited the school—and she realized that many of them were wearing outerwear that was dirty. She recognized that many of them probably didn't have a washer or dryer at home and, when food is scarce, money isn't going to be spent at the laundromat—and they might not have transportation, anyhow.

So, she met with school officials and then raised money to have a washer and dryer installed at the school. She then told the children that she would wash their coats, scarves and mittens for 25 cents while they were in class—and, when someone didn't have 25 cents, she washed them, anyhow.

Before the children would leave for home, Tracy hung up their freshly washed coats in the appropriate school lockers, giving the children a sense of pride.

Writing exercise:

Make a list of what you could do to give others a sense of dignity. Brainstorm as wildly as you'd like and then see if you could put at least one of them into action. Can you write a letter to the editor of your local newspaper that could make a difference for a disenfranchised group of people? Use your writing talents to write a grant application to help an organization get funding? Be creative and use the gifts God has given you to make a difference in the world!

Prayer:

God—please open my eyes so that I can see the need that surrounds me. Help me to trust in your providence, knowing that—if I am truly doing your will—you will empower me. I offer up my prayers for those who are hungry, those who are thirsty. I pray for those who are sick or lonely, for those who are in physical prisons or prisons of their own making. I lift them all to you and ask you to use me to help heal your hurting world. Amen.

Week 26

Because I was hungry, and you gave me something to eat. I was thirsty, and you gave me something to drink. I was a stranger, and you welcomed me. I was naked, and you clothed me. I was sick, and you took care of me. I was in prison, and you visited me. Then the righteous will say to him, 'Lord, when did we see you hungry and give you something to eat, or thirsty and give you something to drink? When did we see you as a stranger and welcome you, or see you naked and clothe you? When did we see you sick or in prison, and visit you?' The king will answer them, 'I tell all of you with certainty, since you did it for one of the least important of these brothers of mine, you did it for me.' (Matthew 25:35-40)

Yep. This verse is important enough to reflect on it for a second week. This week, though, I want to tell you about my friend, Barbie. She was looking out her kitchen window one morning, something she'd done many times before. This time, though, she realized how many people were shivering in the public park that she could see—and, clearly, if they'd had somewhere warm to go, they would have already gone.

This winter was frigid, absolutely miserable—and here were growing numbers of people without shelter. Right outside her window. Now, Barbie doesn't have much money and she needs to pinch pennies. So, she also needed to get creative. She posted a note on Facebook, asking her friends if they'd be willing to donate one blanket to help out a stranger. Just one blanket.

To say that the response was heartwarming would be an understatement. Her message spread and she soon had blankets, scarves, winter coats, gloves and warm socks. Barbie doesn't drive, so some people offered to pick up donations for her. As she received the donations, she gave them to people in the park—and then gave the overage to food distribution centers.

Barbie lost count of how many donations she received, but she knows that it was more than 500 blankets, with approximately 300 winter coats and 1,000 pairs of warm socks.

Look out your own window? Whom do you see? What ministry does God have planned for you?

Writing exercise:

Pull out your list from last week. Add to it as new ideas come up and once again try to find at least one you can put into action. Can you use your writing skills to publish an article or blog post? One that can help spur others to join you in a project where you embrace being your brother's (and sister's) keeper?

Prayer:

Today, God, I want to thank you for Tracy and for Barbie—and for everyone else who sees your hurting children and offers them love in a tangible form. Like Martha who offered hospitality to Jesus, these women (and men!) see a need and don't wait for the "other guy" to take action. Help me to join their numbers to offer food, drink, shelter and more to your children in need. Amen.

Week 27

They went into the house, and when they saw the child with his mother Mary, they knelt down and worshiped him. They brought out their gifts of gold, frankincense, and myrrh, and presented them to him. (Matthew 2:11)

We normally read this Scripture during the Epiphany season, but the reality is that we can and should offer up gifts to God every single day. Here are some ideas:

- Think about someone who makes your life challenging (we all have one—or more!). Pray for this person, asking God to soften your heart towards him or her. Ask God how you can please him in the relationship that's causing you frustration.
- Volunteer at a local program that provides food for the hungry or sign up to become a Big Brother/Big Sister—or find another way that you can give back to the community. Perhaps you can start walking dogs at the local animal protective league and use that time for even more meditation and prayer.
- Find everyday ways to be a humble servant. As just one example, slow down. Open the door to stores for the people behind you, instead of hurrying through, or give up the good parking spot, even though you really were there first. Savor the beauty that surrounds you, all of which was created by God and is intended for your pleasure.
- Forgive. Forgive, whether that means the person who just cut you off in traffic or whether that means someone against whom you've held a longstanding grudge.
- Call someone and offer a much-needed apology, whether it's long overdue or about something more recent.

- When it's tempting to say or do something negative or angry, stop. Breathe. Pray.
- Write a note or visit someone who is a shut in. Let him (or her!) know that he's been in your thoughts and prayers. Offer to go grocery shopping or run other errands. Change a light bulb that's difficult for that person to reach.
- Write a thank you note to your pastor, to a missionary, to the church organist and/or Sunday school teacher. Or to all of the above and more! Who keeps your church clean? Who answers the phones and keeps church records? Who is quietly faithful in attendance every Sunday?
- Say "I love you" to the people in your life. Say it and then show that you mean what you say.

Writing exercise:

I probably don't even need to describe the exercise! Make your own list—and do more than just make a list. Live it out. Every day. When you fall short, know that we all do, and then recommit to living out your list.

Prayer:

God, you have given me the gift of life and there is no way that I could begin to repay you. Yet, I know that it pleases you when I am kind to your other children and when I take care of the animals and Earth that you've created with such loving care. I ask that you accept these actions and gifts as a token of my gratitude. Amen.

Week 28

In the beginning God created the heavens and the earth. (Genesis 1:1)

If you've read any part of the Bible, you've almost surely read that verse. After all, it's human nature and common practice to start reading a book from the beginning. But. Although we might have the best of intentions to keep reading the Bible, we don't always fulfill on our commitment. Perhaps it's because you've gotten busy. Or maybe the Bible is too big or intimidating. Or maybe it's just too hard to understand.

If, however, you can commit to a daily Bible reading program, then the blessings that you'll receive will greatly outweigh the effort that you put in—and you don't need to wait for January 1 to start. Any day is the perfect day to begin.

Having said that, there's nothing wrong with using available resources to make the process manageable, especially if Bible reading is new to you. Consider looking at this website if you'd like to read the Bible in a year's time: https://www.ewordtoday.com/year

This site provides Bible reading plans using more than 50 translations of the Bible, including ones using contemporary language that's easier for modern ears to understand. You can choose how you want to read the Bible, with these options:

- Chronologically: The example given was that Job lived before Abraham was born (I didn't know that . . . something else to look into!), so the chronological reading integrates the Book of Job with Genesis.
- Historically: You can read the books of the Bible according to their estimated date of writing (which doesn't match the order in the Bible itself).

- New then Old: You can read the New Testament first.
- Old then New: You can read the Old Testament first.
- Old and New: Each day includes a passage from each.

If this sounds confusing, don't worry. You simply choose an option and click on the appropriate links and the text is organized for you.

I ultimately went a different route, using an Episcopalian resource titled *The Bible Challenge: Read the Bible in a Year*. You can find this book on Amazon and find out more about this plan at www.thecenterforbiblicalstudies.org. Each day, in *The Bible Challenge*, a different pastor from around the world provides insight into the day's chapters, along with questions to consider and a relevant prayer. This system has you reading a portion of the Old Testament plus one from the New Testament—plus a Psalm—each day.

The bottom line, of course, is that it doesn't matter which system works best for you as long as it helps you to develop a daily habit of Bible reading.

Writing exercise:

If you're struggling to read your Bible daily, try one—or both—of these exercises:

1) Write a letter to someone (it doesn't have to be a real person), sharing why it's important that he or she reads the Bible daily. Be impassioned in your plea!
2) Imagine that you could no longer read a Bible. Perhaps they've all been taken away by some band of evildoers—use your imagination about the specifics. Write about how that changed your life, how it hurt the life of the church. Then, imagine that a Bible has been found! Write about your feelings. A huge sense of relief? A renewed appreciation?

Everything to God in Prayer

Prayer:

God, I praise you for giving us your Word. Please help me understand the messages held within. I ask that, as I read my Bible, you fill me with the Holy Spirit to share your Word with people around me— Christians who need encouragement along with those who have not yet come to Christ. Help me to also remember the words of St. Francis when he said, "Preach the Gospel, always. If necessary, use words." Amen.

Week 29

I myself am convinced, my brothers and sisters, that you yourselves are full of goodness, filled with knowledge and competent to instruct one another. (Romans 15:14)

After I'd written my script for the play, *Sisters Forever: The Burrell Family Letters*, volunteers with a love of theater did a reading of the play to give me feedback. Now, as you writers already know, writing can be a solitary pursuit where you spend a significant amount of time living in your own head. And, I'd lived with these historical characters for two full years, imagining them cooking dinner, visiting family members, finding a new job. I first read twenty years' worth of letters (1929-1949) exchanged among Tempe Burrell and her three grown daughters—Doris, Virginia and Eleanor—and then I wrote the play.

Now, when I was sitting at home writing the script, there were parts that I thought were pretty funny. I even laughed out loud. But, when I sat at the reading, I started to worry that my words weren't humorous at all. Maybe they were in fact amateurish and embarrassing. So, you can imagine my relief when they laughed in the right spots! Whew.

They then gave me two key pieces of advice: one was that I had the characters sitting too much, so to put them into action based on their personalities. Therefore, the consummate volunteer Tempe began rolling bandages for the Red Cross; neat freak Virginia would sweep, dust and straighten out doilies on furniture; Eleanor, the hostess with the most-ess, would serve tea; and Doris would type in her magazine office—and drink bourbon and/or smoke cigarettes more than was probably healthy.

The other piece of advice was to have these women discuss local events in addition to the conversations about national woes during the Great Depression, World War II and the like.

Their feedback for me was fantastic—and I could tell that the advice-givers offered it up in the spirit of wanting the best play possible. And that is what Paul was suggesting, I believe, in his letter to the Romans. Loving guidance. (Other versions of the Bible use the word "admonish" instead of "instruct," which sounds more like scolding in today's lingo.) *Loving guidance.* Not ordering someone else around or criticizing their choices simply because they're different from what you might do. It's a fine line but, when done with Christian love, it's a true blessing.

Writing exercise:

Imagine that a friend from church is causing conflict among her family members and, from your perspective, she is partially at fault. She asks your advice. Write out the specifics of the imaginary situation—and what you would say in response.

Now envision someone from church asking if the two of you can talk—and she kindly but firmly points out that you've hurt her feelings, perhaps even deeply. You are stunned. Create a scenario about this situation and how it is resolved.

Prayer:

God—You have given us a family of fellow Christians, where we can love one another, support one another—and, when necessary, guide and instruct one another through challenging situations. I pray that you give me a discerning spirit and the ability to find the right words when a tough conversation needs to take place. Amen.

Week 30

He has made everything beautiful in its time. He has also set eternity in the human heart; yet no one can fathom what God has done from beginning to end. (Ecclesiastes 3:11)

John Gorski had never thrown a boomerang before, but the guy he just met—Gary Broadbent—was encouraging him to compete in a tournament. John was a strong guy, a black belt in karate, and so John agreed. And did poorly.

The weather was so beautiful, though, that they decided to hold another competition, just for fun—and it was quickly time for John to compete in the maximum time aloft (MTA) event. In MTA, you throw a hockey-stick-shaped boomerang high in the air, hoping to throw it above the thermal where it will make a circle before descending back to earth. (Ever see birds gliding? They're riding the thermal.)

He succeeded in his quest to throw above the thermal, but the boomerang hovered in a single spot for quite a while, just a tiny black dot in the sky. Suddenly, Gary started shouting that John's boomerang had been in the air for more than two minutes—a world record if he caught the descending 'rang!

The boomerang then started its circle, but stopped at the halfway point. Over the Olentangy River, of course. John wanted the world record, so he removed his shoes, socks and shirt. Diving into the river, he tread water underneath his boomerang because they sometimes fall out of the thermal—and then it began the second half of its circle. John scrambled onto land and chased it, barely clothed and covered in green river gunk, with other 'rangers following him with stopwatches, shouting encouragement.

By the time John returned to the boomerang field, it was now the site of a children's soccer game. John pleaded for the referees to stop the game so that he could catch his boomerang (just a tiny dot in the sky, remember!). The ref eventually agreed, "probably for the safety of the children," John suspects, reminding us about how odd he probably looked.

The boomerang finally descended—and John caught it, setting a new world record in maximum time aloft: 17 minutes and six seconds. "God held the boomerang," John told me in one of the interviews I've done with him, "until he was ready to return it to me."

God's timing. We can't predict it and we certainly don't always understand it. But, as faithful Christians, we need to remember that God's timing is perfect in all things, given the perspective of eternity. Not all of our stories about divine timing will be as dramatic as John's, of course, but our lives are all governed by this heavenly stopwatch.

Writing exercise:

Think about when you wanted something—a certain job or person as a spouse—and, later on, you realized that those weren't the right fits for you, anyhow. How do you see God's timing at work? In what ways are you struggling today to accept God's timing? Does reflecting upon past situations help you to trust God in today's challenging moments? Write honestly about how you really feel, not how you *think* you should feel. God can meet you wherever you are.

Prayer:

God, I thank you for the "big" moments in life when your handiwork is clearly shown to me, as well as the everyday moments. Help me to accept and trust in your timing, to fit myself into your rhythms instead of trying to be in charge of what happens in my life, when. I ask that you meet where I am, today, and guide me to where you want me to be. Amen.

Week 31

We have different gifts, according to the grace given to each of us. If your gift is prophesying, then prophesy in accordance with your faith; if it is serving, then serve; if it is teaching, then teach; if it is to encourage, then give encouragement; if it is giving, then give generously; if it is to lead, do it diligently; if it is to show mercy, do it cheerfully. (Romans 12:6-8)

My guess is that some of you have been given the gifts needed for writing devotionals. And, this week, I'd like to encourage you to try writing one. Here are steps that I recommend:

1) Pray for God's guidance as you write and ask him to lead you to the appropriate message to deliver.
2) Choose a Bible verse (or a couple of verses) for your devotional that fit at least one of these categories:
   a. among your favorites
   b. appropriate for a situation you want to write about
   c. part of a set of writer's guidelines (if you want to try to publish)
   d. relevant for your target audience (teens? busy mothers? people who are chronically ill? inmates in a prison?)
3) Or, you can use a Bible concordance tool to enter a theme or topic (shame, forgiveness, water) to see what verses come up—and then choose the best verse(s) to use for your devotional. Concordances often also contain dictionaries, encyclopedias, a thesaurus and other helpful tools, and often allow you to choose from multiple versions of the Bible if you want to compare and contrast.
4) Read the verses before and after this section of the Bible to make sure that you understand the context.

5) If you need more clarification about these verses, talk to your minister or priest (or other clergy) and/or read what theologians have written about them.
6) Think of a situation that these Bible verses can speak to; this can be from:
   a. your own life
   b. the lives of people you know
   c. the news
7) What role did God play in that situation?
8) Not all devotionals will fit this formula, but it's a good starting point: write 100-400 words of the personal or news story, only including the points that are relevant to the devotional. It can be a temptation to include too much and it's an art form to choose precisely the right details.
9) Use the next 100-300 words to connect the Bible verse, your anecdote and the point you'd like to make about the Scripture. How would this verse and your anecdote help others with a challenge in their own lives?
10) Consider including a couple of questions that the reader might want to think about, especially as to how it pertains to his or her own life.
11) End with a relevant prayer.
12) Put the devotional away for a while and then read it again, to do any necessary rewriting or editing.

Note: See appendix I for tips on publishing your devotion.

Prayer:

God, thank you for giving me a love of words and of writing. I ask that you inspire me to share the message that you want me to share, and guide me into delivering it to the people who need to hear it most. As I write a devotional, let me put aside all ego and pride, and focus on sharing your Good News in a way that will connect with other people. Not my will, but thy will be done as I write them. Amen.

Week 32

Whoever believes in me, as Scripture has said, rivers of living water will flow from within them. (John 7:38)

I spent four pleasurable years serving as the managing editor of a magazine publishing company. One of our publications was a full-color print magazine that shared intriguing family-friendly activities to enjoy in Northeast Ohio. I wrote some of the content and would often take my young children with me to see what they liked about a place before I wrote about the locale.

One day, we traveled to the Seneca Caverns in Bellevue, Ohio—which is one of the region's largest underground caverns. As we toured the cavern, we traveled through seven different levels, each one taking us further underground. Nearer the surface, the rooms seemed spacious enough but, as we descended, the area grew tighter and I envisioned the cavern as having a womb-like shape.

By the time we'd traveled downward about 110 feet, we could glimpse and hear Ole Mist'ry River, described on the website of this attraction as the "crystal clear flowing stream which is part of the vast ground-water system."

I found this experience totally fascinating and, shortly afterwards, utterly and claustrophobically terrifying in retrospect. And now, with the perspective of time, I envision this journey as an analogy for when we travel deep within ourselves to meet up with the living waters of God.

It isn't easy to access this part of ourselves, perhaps impossible to do so fully. Some people approach this part of themselves through meditation or centering prayer, and I suspect that we can catch wispy corners of this part of our selves when we dream. And, ideally, this is the direction that we want to travel when we apply ourselves to the discipline of spiritual writing.

Kelly Boyer Sagert

Writing exercise:

I wish that I could lay out a clear path for you to travel to this state of being, but I can't. I can recognize when I'm closer to it and know when it's frustratingly out of reach. The process involves stilling yourself so that you can disconnect from the strictly intellectual activities that are useful for practical activities but can serve as roadblocks in your spiritual journey.

Here is one practice to try. Adapt to what works for you.

I have a few sets of Anglican prayer beads, which each consist of thirty-three beads. There are four groups of beads; each group has a larger bead and seven smaller ones; the 33rd "bead" is really a cross. As I touch each of the beads, with my eyes closed, I breathe deeply in and out. When I touch a larger bead, I focus on part of Psalm 46:10: *Be still and know that I am God.* Then, as I touch each of the smaller beads and deeply breathe, I "say" these words in my brain: *I am listening.*

Consider doing some version of this exercise and then writing about your experiences, accepting that all comes to you in God's timing.

Prayer:

God, thank you for allowing me to come to you in prayer, no matter where I am geographically, no matter my state of mind or focus, and no matter where I am on my spiritual path towards you. Refresh me with your living waters so that I can serve you in the way that you have planned, caring for your other children and witnessing the Good News. Amen.

Week 33

This text appeared in *Ruby for Women*—and so the Scripture, writing exercise and prayer appear in the text in a different order from other weeks in this book.

God communicates with his people (us!) through covenants, including the Covenant of Grace where he solemnly promises salvation through atonement: the sacrifice of Jesus on the cross and then his resurrection. And, when God makes a promise, he keeps it eternally.

To deepen your commitment to God, consider making a sacred covenant with him. Of course, as fallible human beings, we make heartfelt promises but often fail in carrying them out—and that should be acknowledged in your covenant. This is not a covenant between equals, but between you and the one who gives life and breath.

Here is one process to creating a covenant:

1) Choose a Bible verse that resonates with you.
2) Pray about it and allow time for listening to God's response.
3) Write your covenant to God, acknowledging your fallibility in keeping your promises.
4) If need be, put the writing away and review it later, to make sure you have created an authentic covenant that truly expresses your intent.
5) Read the promise out loud to God.
6) Know that you can make changes if you don't feel that you're expressing your deepest intentions yet.
7) When you are satisfied with your covenant: meditate, either in silence or with spiritual music playing softly in the background

8) Then, envision yourself lifting the covenant up to God and asking Him to place it in your heart.

Here's what I've come up with:

"For we are the product of His hand, heaven's poetry etched on lives, created in Jesus, the Liberator, to accomplish the good works God arranged long ago." (Ephesians 2:10)

God—you have blessed me beyond measure and I want to make the rest of my life a thank you note to you. I am so grateful.

You have drenched me with love, grace, mercy, compassion and forgiveness, and I humbly pray that you teach me how to share what you have so freely given me with others. Let it overflow, God, let it overflow.

I want to live according to the divine purpose that you have designed especially for me and I want to witness for you. Help me to be your hands and feet on earth, Lord. Help me to be your heart and tongue as I share how you have transformed my life. Show me how to be a light for you, God, show me how.

Reveal to me how I can become a person who prays without ceasing. Help me to create the spiritual white space needed for contemplation and prayer.

Let me dive into the pool of joy that comes with communion with you, let me empty myself out in an act of blessed humility so that you can fill me with the Holy Spirit.

This is the covenant of my imperfect intentions, Lord. Support and guide me each time that I fall short, and correct me when I drift off course, so that I can grow closer to you.

I love you. Amen.

Week 34

Therefore do not worry about tomorrow, for tomorrow will worry about itself. Each day has enough trouble of its own. (Matthew 6:34)

During my two days with the Sisters of St. Francis of Sylvania, I spent a goodly amount of time outdoors in the prayer gardens, one in particular. This garden featured a statue of Saint Clare of Assisi, who was one of the first followers of St. Francis. In fact, she was said to be with Francis when he died. She founded the Order of Poor Ladies, a Franciscan religious order, writing the first monastic rule known to be written by a woman. The order was renamed the Order of Saint Clare, often called the Poor Clares.

Her statue in Sylvania was surrounded by gorgeous flowers with a bench nearby. While sitting on the bench, I watched a lightning bug patiently crawl up one side of a blade of grass and then just as patiently (at least the creature *seemed* patient!) crawl down. Then up and down another blade. And another. As I watched, I wondered why the little guy didn't just *fly*. It would be so much quicker! Why, in the amount of time he crawled just ONE blade of grass, he could be— well, he could be . . . well, at a blade of grass that was further away!

At that point, I realized something that may already be apparent to many of you: just because I—or another creature—CAN rush, it doesn't mean that it's always the best thing to do. For the lightning bug, the grass a few feet away apparently wasn't perceived as greener than the blade of his current focus.

Plus, that lightning bug was focused on what was happening now, not worrying about the height of a blade of grass a few inches away. It can be hard for me to focus on the present, to not worry. But we are called to trust in God and to focus on each day as it comes. Easy? No. Again, it's a journey.

Writing exercise:

Focus on free writing about what is happening around you right now, using as many senses as you can incorporate. When you take a sip of your coffee or tea, for example, write about what it feels like on your tongue, as it slips down your throat. What music is playing? Or what birds are singing? Is the sun warm on your shoulders? Can you feel the smooth sensation of paper beneath your hand? When you're done with this exercise—try not to hurry!—what have you learned about focusing on the present? How can you apply this to your daily life?

Prayer:

God—Help me to focus on each day as it comes and to trust in your providence. Help me to turn my worries over to you, knowing that all will happen according to your plan and in your timing. Help me to focus on the present, and to enjoy the beauty and face the challenges that you have laid out for my day. Amen.

Week 35

Then Peter came to Jesus and asked, "Lord, how many times shall I forgive my brother or sister who sins against me? Up to seven times?" Jesus answered, "I tell you, not seven times, but seventy-seven times." (Matthew 18:21-22)

A friend of mine once asked her elementary-school-aged daughter to go upstairs and throw the towels down the laundry chute. (How many of you still have and use laundry chutes?) Her daughter complied—and soon there were more towels in the basement than my friend expected. She investigated and then realized that she hadn't requested that her daughter toss the *dirty* towels down the chute—only "the towels"—and so the girl emptied the cabinet of all clean towels and sent them down to the basement.

This was a simple misunderstanding and I laughed when my friend shared this anecdote. But, many times in life, misunderstandings fester in darker ways. And yet, people find a way to forgive.

Gary is one such man. When a man named Tom drove drunk and killed Gary's wife and two children in an accident, Gary visited Tom in prison. He asked Tom how his children were doing—but Tom didn't really know, since his under-aged son wasn't allowed in the prison. News stories report that Gary offered to try to help Tom's children heal while their father serves 19 to 30 years in prison for three counts of second-degree murder. He also formally agreed to not try to block any attempts for early release.

When Teresa's son was murdered by someone robbing their home, she made a victim statement in court. She told the judge that she and her son's father forgave the perpetrator because that's what Jesus commanded, adding that their first prayers were for the murderer.

Could I forgive to that degree? I can't imagine. And yet, people such as Gary and Teresa show that it's possible to live up to the commandment, forgiving in the direst of circumstances and shining a guiding light for others. Do their actions make it easier for you to forgive lesser sins and transgressions?

Writing exercise:

Think of someone who has wronged you. Free write what would happen if you did forgive this person. What would you gain? Would you lose anything? Do you imagine that NOT forgiving someone is giving you a sense of control over a painful situation? If so, is that really true?

Now, reverse the situation and imagine that YOU had committed the action that you find hard to forgive. Free write how you would want that other person to respond to you. When you're done, are there any actions that you intend to take?

Prayer:

God—I ask for a forgiving spirit, both for significant wrongs done to me and for the smaller ones that build up and become irritants. When I struggle to forgive, help me to remember the sacrifice that you made for me in the crucifixion. When I wrong someone else, help me to ask forgiveness and to make appropriate amends. Amen.

Week 36

Therefore confess your sins to each other and pray for each other so that you may be healed. The prayer of a righteous person is powerful and effective. (James 5:16)

One day, I found a bag containing four boomerangs at the top of my bookcase. *The good news: they were gorgeous! The bad news: they weren't mine!*

I immediately recognized them as unique creations of Alan Scott Craig, a gifted boomerang artist whom I'd interviewed when writing my book, *About Boomerangs: America's Silent Sport*. After the book came out, I had called Alan and suggested that I interview him for potential magazine articles, and so he loaned me samples of his work for inspiration and reference.

Problem: I'd never followed through on that interview.

It might not seem like a big deal. I could just return the boomerangs, right? Well, Alan had sent those boomerangs to me *seventeen years ago.* Yes. Seventeen. How on earth would I even find him?

Fortunately, he was on LinkedIn. Whew. Problem solved?

Of course not. What on earth could I say to him after I'd kept his high-quality boomerangs for nearly two decades?? For almost 6,000 days???

I nervously typed "Long Overdue Apology" in the LinkedIn subject line and then explained to Alan that I was very sorry for keeping his boomerangs and that, while I hoped he'd believe that it wasn't intentional, it was 100% my fault. After I sent the message, I figured he'd either ignore me or be angry. I looked forward to neither, but preferred the second so we could at least come to some sort of resolution, even if not ideal.

He responded almost immediately and I expected him to be upset. Instead, he accepted my apology without reservation and said that he kept himself too busy fixing his own mistakes to have time left over to fuss over mine. He added that, if he had cash for every time his mouth promised something his body didn't do, he'd have a whole lot of spending money. He then . . . ready for this? He asked when I wanted to schedule the interview!

I was stunned by his graciousness and we have since begun coauthoring a Christian book together. Who would have thought?

Now, my situation was pretty clear cut. I had totally goofed in keeping the boomerangs. And, thanks to Alan' response, the resolution was equally as clear cut. But, many situations are muddier. In those cases, if you might need to ask for forgiveness, it helps to remember that attempting to restore a relationship is far more important than sorting out minute details about what was—or wasn't—"really" your fault.

Writing exercise:

Although asking for forgiveness in person is ideal, it isn't always possible. Alan, for example, lives in California and I live in Ohio. And, if it's too difficult to face someone and admit you were wrong, sending a letter or email is far better than doing nothing and has the advantage of giving you time to carefully craft your message. What letter or email (or notes for an in-person conversation) should you write today?

Prayer:

God, convict my heart when there are wrongs that I need to right. Guide me in finding the right words to use to acknowledge my fault and to do my best to make amends. We are all imperfect beings and need the guidance of Scripture to help us restore relationships in a way that pleases you. Lead us, God! Amen.

Week 37

"You are the light of the world. A town built on a hill cannot be hidden. Neither do people light a lamp and put it under a bowl. Instead they put it on its stand, and it gives light to everyone in the house. In the same way, let your light shine before others, that they may see your good deeds and glorify your Father in heaven. (Matthew 5:14-16)

In one scene from my play, *Freedom's Light: A Stop Along the Underground Railroad*, a character named Pepper Jack is waving about a drinking gourd that he uses to gather drinking water from the creek. During one performance, part of the gourd broke off, and went flying through the air, knocking over a tree prop. Pepper Jack, standing up there in the bright lights of the stage, couldn't have a do-over, so he ad-libbed a line about the quality of gourds these days and kept the storyline going.

Some of the actors worried that I would be upset, but I was just relieved that I wasn't the one standing up on that stage, having to keep the play momentum going when all didn't go as planned. I'd much rather be the one doing research than the one rehearsing. I'd much rather be the one writing the play, not the one having to memorize all of those lines. I'd much rather be the one who can edit my work in the privacy of my own home, not the one who is performing and needs to modify on-the-fly (in this case, literally after something unexpectedly flew across the stage!).

Interestingly enough, several actors have told me they're glad they aren't the ones having to do the researching, the writing and the editing! Let's face it. We're all different. God made some of us the ones who thrive in the spotlight—and that's great. Others of us are more solitary—and, others like me, fall somewhere in between.

What's most important is to follow the path that God has created for you personally, which can take plenty of prayer, reflection and courage to determine. Each one of us has a light to shine in the world, whether that's literally true or symbolically so.

Writing exercise:

No matter how introverted or extroverted God made you, it surely must give him great pleasure when you let your light shine by showing love, mercy and compassion to others, especially when no one else will ever know. Make a list of ways that you can do that in your everyday life. If you have trouble getting started, check out the lists of random acts of kindness found online.

Prayer:

God, I am fearfully and wonderfully made, created in a way that allows me to shine my light as a witness for you. Help me find ways this week to show love, kindness, mercy and compassion to people I know and to the strangers that I meet. Show me the opportunities, God. Forgive me when I don't see them or I don't follow through, and empower me to try again. Amen.

Week 38

Let no corrupting talk come out of your mouths, but only such as is good for building up, as fits the occasion, that it may give grace to those who hear. And do not grieve the Holy Spirit of God, by whom you were sealed for the day of redemption. Let all bitterness and wrath and anger and clamor and slander be put away from you, along with all malice. Be kind to one another, tenderhearted, forgiving one another, as God in Christ forgave you. (Ephesians 4:29-32)

The greatest wisdom of all is found in the Scriptures—and then God also gives wisdom to others to help guide us on the right path. Here's one example of down-to-earth advice that's hard to debate:

"No matter how busy you get, you are NEVER too busy to use good manners or good grammar." (Beatrice "Nana" Boyer)

My grandmother received her diploma from Akron State University in the 1920s with a degree in literature. Not too many women were getting bachelor degrees in that era and she took hers seriously. She took good manners even *more* seriously—and, if she didn't get a thank you note quickly after she'd sent me a gift, she would write me a letter asking the reason why!

She could be pretty stern when manners were on the line, but she was also quite encouraging. When I was in elementary school, she'd ask me to read to her out loud, telling me that I had a "beautiful reading voice." Now, in reality, I'm not sure that was true outside the ears of a loving grandmother—but her words gave me the confidence that I (as a shy child) needed. We'd then analyze the characters and dissect the plot, and I credit this as one building block of my love of reading and writing.

One day, when we arrived for a visit, she greeted me at the door, her face shining. "Your timing is perfect!" she said. "In a few hours, a documentary will debut about King Henry VIII and Anne Boleyn!" I still remember the dramatic moment of Anne's execution and I credit my grandmother's enthusiasm as one building block of my love of history.

Another evening, she sat and listened to the Cleveland Indians with me on the radio. She clapped whenever I cheered and would say, "I have no idea what's going on, but you look happy so it must be good!" I credit this joyousness as a building block to my being willing to step outside of my comfort zone (not always, but on occasion!).

So hard and yet so simple: *be kind to one another.*

Writing exercise:

Create a list of three people who might need extra kindness right now (and these might be the people to whom it's tough to extend compassion and encouragement!). Write a note to each one, cheering him or her on. And, if you can, send your note to that person. Even if you don't get a response, you may have changed a life.

Prayer:

God, help me to focus on what really matters in life. Give me the eyes to see and the ears to hear the needs of people around me and show me the way to lighten their burdens. Forgive me when I allow busyness to serve as an excuse and help me to focus each day on priorities—YOUR priorities. Amen.

Week 39

Jesus answered: "Don't you know me, Philip, even after I have been among you such a long time? Anyone who has seen me has seen the Father. How can you say, 'Show us the Father'? Don't you believe that I am in the Father, and that the Father is in me? The words I say to you I do not speak on my own authority. Rather, it is the Father, living in me, who is doing his work. Believe me when I say that I am in the Father and the Father is in me; or at least believe on the evidence of the works themselves. (John 14:9-11)

Continuing the saga of Nana for another week, she also introduced me to one of the most amazing writers ever—and to a genre that I still love: Agatha Christie and the mystery novel.

When I was ten, Nana told me that I was old enough to start reading one of her Agatha Christie books. It was quickly apparent that Christie was a master of her craft, planting clues in plain sight but scattering enough red herrings that you'd look over *here* when you should have been looking over *there*—and vice versa.

After I read several of her novels and then returned home, I was hooked and craved more. So, my father took me to the Lorain Public Library to ask Nancy, the librarian, if I could have an adult library card. *An Adult Library Card.* Oh, my goodness.

I'll never forget how kind Nancy was, telling me that she trusted me to use the adult library appropriately. She showed me where to find the Agatha Christie books (so many!) and then recommended other mystery novelists I might enjoy (there were MORE mystery novelists??? My brain was ready to short circuit with happiness!).

I've continued to read dozens of mystery novels each year, ever since, and love them just as much. You'd therefore think that I would be good at figuring out whodunit. But, you know what? I'm downright lousy, but that's okay because then I get to enjoy each novel to its end!

I can therefore sympathize with Philip, who struggled to understand the interconnectedness among the Father, Son and Holy Spirit. That is one heck of a mystery! And, if we can't figure it out, that's okay. I don't believe that God expects us to understand all of the intricacies during our human lifetimes, only to trust and believe and love. Someday, in heaven, all of the pieces will fit together. In the meantime, there is a whole lot of living to do here on Earth, as God's hands of mercy and voice of love.

Writing exercise:

Surely you have questions of God. Picture yourself sitting next to Jesus, having his undivided attention. Where are you? At a beach? In a coffee shop? In church? What else do you see, hear and smell? What questions do you have of him? How are you feeling? Free write!

Prayer:

God, your depth and breadth, your power, majesty and glory are more than we can fathom. Help us to understand what we need to know to do your will and then let us enjoy the grand mystery of you as Father, Son and Holy Spirit as we live out our lifetimes in service to you. Amen.

Week 40

Therefore, I urge you, brothers and sisters, in view of God's mercy, to offer your bodies as a living sacrifice, holy and pleasing to God—this is your true and proper worship. Do not conform to the pattern of this world, but be transformed by the renewing of your mind. Then you will be able to test and approve what God's will is—his good, pleasing and perfect will. (Romans 12:1-2)

Whenever I've written a play, the most exciting moment occurs on opening night, right before the play debuts for the very first time. For my first play, I'd seen plenty of rehearsals ahead of time; for my third, I never saw one single one of them—and, the middle play? Somewhere in between. But, on opening night, none of that matters. There is a sense of anticipation that absolutely electrifies the air for anyone who has been intimately involved in the play's creation.

I'm not sure that I can fully describe the surreal feeling that takes place when lines that existed only in my head for months, even years, are now being spoken out loud by other people—in front of still other people! That play is thereby christened, using the secular definition of the term.

In a religious sense, at least in the Presbyterian tradition, you are only literally christened—baptized—once, although you remember and reconfirm your baptismal promises when you are confirmed and when others are baptized. You do the same if you become an elder or deacon. When I was given a new lease on life after my series of colon surgeries, though, there wasn't a specific sacrament that corresponded with my second chance at life.

So, I've created my own recommitment and renewal ceremony on a day that I now call Rededication Day. I've decided to celebrate it annually on July 5th, which was the date of my emergency surgery.

On the first anniversary, I didn't do much more than meditate on where I'd been and where I hoped to go in my bonus years. On the second year, I decided that I needed something more concrete—and, fortunately, the mini-pilgrimage with the Sisters of St. Francis took place on that weekend.

My story isn't your story, of course—and yours isn't mine. But I suspect that we all have a pivotal day in our lives that could serve as Rededication Day. Right?

Writing exercise:

What day is your Rededication Day? It could be related to a health challenge or another sort of crisis, or it could be the day of something especially wonderful—the day you got married or became a parent. Or it could be the day that you committed your life to Christ. No matter what it is, free write about that day. What would be your ideal way to recommit yourself to God on that day each year? Don't limit yourself to practicalities just yet. After you're done, then write about more practical ways that you can recommit yourself to God the next time that day of the year arrives.

Prayer:

God—you are with me every day, even when I am not aware of your presence—and, for that, I am extremely grateful. But, some days are more imbued with meaning than others, and I have chosen [name specifics] as my Rededication Day. On this day, I [list your own specifics]. Amen.

Week 41

How much better to get wisdom than gold, to get insight rather than silver! (Proverbs 16:16)

Chet Snouffer is a ten-time national boomerang champion for the United States and a three-time world champion. He is known as the Michael Jordan of the boomerang world for his domination of the sport and for his longevity at the top. He has astonished many a spectator by throwing a boomerang, then performing a standing back flip—and then calmly catching the 'rang behind his back. And that was when he was just warming up.

He's also a good guy, having served as the children's outreach pastor at church and otherwise volunteering his time for causes that matter.

One day, he was demonstrating throwing techniques for a group of young children, including his son. After dazzling the spectators, he threw an especially valuable boomerang known as a "Jonas." When he threw that priceless 'rang, though, it didn't come back (something quite unusual for Chet)! Instead, it flew over a rocky and hilly area full of thorns. Frustrated, he looked over the edge of the rocks. No boomerang. So, he drove his car over to the spot and turned on the headlights. Still, nothing.

He then climbed down through the rocks, getting increasingly frustrated at the futility of his search. He finally sat down on a rock, dropped his head into his hands, and vented about his rotten luck. Life was so unfair! Here he was, donating his own time, something he certainly didn't NEED to do—and he loses a precious belonging! Just not right.

After fuming for a while, though, he began to feel sheepish. There was his bright-eyed son, waiting for him to return to the boomerang demonstration—and his wife and daughter whom he cherished, waiting at home to see him. He made a living doing what he loved and was full of good health. He didn't have rotten luck at all . . . in fact, he was blessed beyond measure!

Chet then lifted his head—and there, right at his feet, was the boomerang. "That gave me chills," Chet told me. "It wasn't until I acknowledged what was really important that God allowed me to have my boomerang back."

Writing exercise:

Even though Chet is a faithful Christian, he can still get distracted from his priorities—as can we all. Free write a list of what keeps you from focusing on what matters most. Is it your job? Worries and anxieties? Prized possessions? After you free write, ask yourself which of those issues deserve more attention than God. More than the people that God has blessed you with in life? How will your answers change how you live each day?

Prayer:

God—give me eyes to see and ears to hear, and give me the wisdom to discern what is truly important in my life. Help me to understand where my focus should be throughout the day. Forgive me when I become so accustomed to the blessings in my life that I no longer perceive them—and allow me to see them anew with fresh eyes. Amen.

Week 42

What shall we say, then? Shall we go on sinning so that grace may increase? By no means! We are those who have died to sin; how can we live in it any longer? Or don't you know that all of us who were baptized into Christ Jesus were baptized into his death? We were therefore buried with him through baptism into death in order that, just as Christ was raised from the dead through the glory of the Father, we too may live a new life. (Romans 6:1-4)

Those of you who write for income on a freelance basis, whether part time or full, know that looking for your next gig can occupy lots of your time. Sometimes, to get the assignment, you need to be creative while remaining honest. Here's an example. I saw a publisher advertising for a funeral director who was also a freelance writer to author a book about how to become a funeral director. I emailed the publisher, letting her know that I was a freelance writer and author, while my father was a longtime funeral director who offered to work with me on the project. And, I got the job! So, I wrote about the professionals who care for the dead and minister to their families.

As Christians, we can live with the freedom of knowing that we will be alive in Christ again after death, which is a joyous thought, indeed! But, our earthly bodies first must die. The Reverend Lou Will, who graciously wrote the foreword in this book, has suggested that we think about our own funerals ahead of time. What Scriptures would we want read? What hymns sung?

As for me, I know I want the hymn, *Amazing Grace*—for many reasons. One is that I love the hymn so much that I even had it sung at my wedding as guests were waiting for me to walk down the aisle. Another is that the promise that grace hath brought me safe thus far is so true—as is this marvelous gift: that grace will lead me (and you!) home.

Yet a third reason . . . the story about the songwriter is so compelling. John Newton was raised as a Christian by his mother but, when she died in his childhood, her influence appeared to disappear. He was forced into the British Royal Navy in 1744, but he persuaded his superiors to release him to work on a slave trading ship, which he did for many years. When a storm hit, he somewhat returned to his Christian beliefs, but later admitted he wasn't yet a full believer. Ultimately, he fully committed to the faith, becoming ordained into Anglican ministry. In that role, he and poet William Cowper wrote many hymns, one of which is *Amazing Grace.*

Writing exercise:

What Scriptures and/or hymns would you like to be part of your funeral service? Why? Free write about what these choices mean to you. How does that change how you live today?

Prayer:

God—I thank you for all of the blessings in my life and for the sure assurance that life will not end with the death of my earthly body. Instead, we are promised life eternal because we have been born again in Christ. Help me to embrace that promise and share it with others who need to hear the good news! Amen.

Week 43

For now we see only a reflection as in a mirror; then we shall see face to face. Now I know in part; then I shall know fully, even as I am fully known. (I Corinthians 13:12)

My hometown—Lorain, Ohio—is known as the International City in honor of the large numbers of immigrants who settled here because of manufacturing jobs in steel, ship building, auto assembly and more. Although many manufacturing plants have closed or shrunk in size, Lorain remains rich in ethnic and cultural diversity.

One well known Lorain native who takes pride in this diversity is Nobel Prize-winning and Pulitzer Prize-winning author, Toni Morrison. She has also been awarded the Presidential Medal of Freedom—and so our city is justifiably proud of Morrison, as well, naming the reading room at the Lorain Public Library's main branch after her.

In 2015, the library decided to decorate the reading room with a mosaic. They contracted with a mosaic artist but, rather than having her create the artwork, she oversaw the efforts of community members who came in to each create their own small sections of the mosaic.

My son, Ryan, and I participated. While you were working on the mosaic, all you could focus on was your own little area of blue or green or brown, intently gluing your shattered pieces next to other broken pieces. But, if you climbed the stairs to the second story of the library, you could begin to see the formation of the waves of lake water, the expansiveness of the sky, the gleaming of the sun.

You could see people enjoying a boat ride down Lorain's Black River, smile at the birds soaring above the Bascule Bridge—and appreciate the open book added to the mosaic as a reminder that books connect us to our world. In other words, the jagged pieces/parts began to look like a full picture from this higher perspective.

Think how wonderful it would be if, in life in general, all you needed to do was take a few steps back or climb a set of stairs to see the full picture! Think how many hurt feelings this could prevent, how many arguments it could save, how many dead ends you could avoid. But, unfortunately, it's not that simple. The reality is that only God can see all. The challenge, then, is to continue to develop trust in God, even when life isn't going well, relying on fellow Christians for support—and then supporting other people whenever you can.

Writing exercise:

Create your own word mosaic! You can do this by buying a poetry magnet set where individual words are printed on small magnets or other similar products where words or phrases are printed on slips of paper. Or, you can create your own set. No matter which version you use, choose several magnets or slips of paper without looking at the imprinted words. Then meditate on this week's Bible verse before free writing the story of your mosaic using the words you've selected as inspiration.

Prayer:

God—sometimes events in my life and in our world don't seem to make sense, including [list examples that are heavy on your heart right now]. Help me to remember that you hold the future and that, in this lifetime, I will only know in part. Give me the patience and grace needed to accept that reality—knowing that, when I am with you in heaven, I will finally know in full. Amen.

Week 44

Therefore if you have any encouragement from being united with Christ, if any comfort from his love, if any common sharing in the Spirit, if any tenderness and compassion, then make my joy complete by being like-minded, having the same love, being one in spirit and of one mind. Do nothing out of selfish ambition or vain conceit. Rather, in humility value others above yourselves, not looking to your own interests but each of you to the interests of the others. (Philippians 2: 1-4)

I was a young mother of two when I began freelancing for our local newspaper. I covered school board and city council meetings. I wrote about mud ordinances. About whether or not it made sense to tear down a water tower that was no longer a viable part of a city's water system but served as a symbol for its residents. You get my drift.

One day, my editor offered me a chance to write a full page, full color feature of a fascinating resident of the county! I was thrilled and wanted this person's name, ASAP. "You're the journalist," he deadpanned in response. "You tell *me* who you think should be profiled." *My mind went blank. Nobody came to mind. My big chance—and I had absolutely nothing to say.*

I feared that my writing career—my fragile fledgling writing career—was already ending. He gave me a couple more days to come up with someone—but I couldn't.

Right before my deadline, I was volunteering at our church's vacation Bible school and our pastor's wife, Sharon, noticed that I looked sad. I explained my predicament—and she simply said, "Well, why don't you interview Gary Broadbent?" Gary, she explained, was an international boomerang champion and he owned the world's largest boomerang collection. Better yet, her son Jason had his phone number!

I contacted Gary and profiled him (and we're friends to this day!). The editor liked it so well that I began writing regular Sunday features. I sold boomerang stories to magazines and this led to the publishing of my first book, my first encyclopedia assignment and more. It was . . . transformational. So, it's reasonable to say that, if I hadn't had the support of the Smucker family early in my career, I might not be writing this book! Therefore, *Everything to God in Prayer* is dedicated to them.

The Reverend Jim Smucker became our pastor in January 1988, and he and his wife—and children Jason, Kirsten and Nathan—have been an integral part of my life and my faith journey. When I was in a crisis situation, Reverend Smucker offered calming words of wisdom. He baptized our children and taught their confirmation classes. He asked me to lead a Christmas Eve church service, sermon included, and otherwise gave me countless opportunities to stretch my wings in the life of our church.

Their entire family is a model of Christian love, compassion and humility. Even when I had doubts and crises of faith, they remained caring and supportive, accepting me for who I was and where I was in my life.

Thank you. Just . . . thank you.

Writing exercise:

Imagine that you are writing a dedication for a book that you just wrote. What is the book's title? How does the dedication read? Why? (And, why aren't you writing that book???)

Prayer:

God—thank you for the encouraging people that you have placed in my life. Too often, I take them for granted. Please jostle me out of my complacency so that I can thank them—and so that I can serve to encourage someone else who may be drifting away from the light. Amen.

Week 45

Ask and it will be given to you; seek and you will find; knock and the door will be opened to you. (Matthew 7:7)

If you believe, you will receive whatever you ask for in prayer. (Matthew 21:22)

Therefore I tell you, whatever you ask for in prayer, believe that you have received it, and it will be yours. (Mark 11:24)

And I will do whatever you ask in my name, so that the Father may be glorified in the Son. You may ask me for anything in my name, and I will do it. (John 14:13-14)

The Bible has plenty to say on the subject of prayer—and the verses listed for this week's devotional are just the tip of the iceberg. Prayer is at the core of the Christian experience—and so, in the spiritual writing classes that we've been holding at our church, we typically close with a prayer. I usually ask if anyone would like to start the prayer (and, so far, someone has always volunteered!) and then anyone who'd like to add something is free to do so, with no pressure to participate.

One especially touching moment happened when Susan, a friend of mine, responded to my request for someone to be a prayer-starter with something like: "I've always been very nervous about praying out loud." I was preparing myself to remind her that there was no pressure—but I'm glad I didn't because she continued in this manner: "But I'd like to now."

Later, she shared these thoughts with me: that the workshops did more than help her to express her spirituality through writing. They also taught her that she didn't need to fear it. "In my family," she said, "spirituality was a taboo subject, not to be discussed or shared." But, the loving environment created by the people in the class "drew stories and truth from my soul that I had forgotten existed. It was the first time I had prayed out loud since I was a little girl in Sunday School."

In retrospect, of course, I shudder to think how I nearly stopped this wonderful event by interrupting Susan to tell her that she didn't need to pray! Many times, the greatest gift you can give someone else is to NOT talk, to just let the person finish his or her thoughts.

Writing exercise:

In the workshop itself, we each work on the same writing exercise and then we go around the circle to discuss the experience. This is the covenant that we follow:

We agree that:

1) Everyone's stories are important. Please participate to the fullest of your ability.
2) Respect is crucial, which includes:
   a. Listening to others
   b. Not judging them
   c. Keeping confidentiality
3) No one will ever be "forced" into sharing what he or she has written.

Are you feeling called to start a similar workshop in your area? Feel free to use or modify the covenant—and to contact me at kbsagert@aol.com for free resources to help make that happen.

Prayer:

Our Father, who art in heaven,
Hallowed be thy name.

Everything to God in Prayer

Thy kingdom come.
Thy will be done in earth,
As it is in heaven.
Give us this day our daily bread.
And forgive us our debts,
As we forgive our debtors.
Lead us not into temptation,
But deliver us from evil.
For thine is the kingdom,
The power, and the glory forever,
Amen.

Week 46

Set a guard over my mouth, Lord; keep watch over the door of my lips. (Psalm 141:3)

Last week, I shared how I almost interrupted my friend, Susan, right when she was ready to pray aloud for the first time in decades. This week, I'm going to share another story where I really needed to *just stop talking*.

It was in the early 1990s and I was barely published. But, boy, did I want to be! So, I decided to attend my first writer's conference—the Midwest Writers Conference in Canton, Ohio. I was able to sign up for a ten-minute one-on-one time with Linda, the editor of *Ohio Writer*, so I went to the library and devoured every single issue of the magazine so that I could speak knowledgeably about its contents. I created a resume to share with her that highlighted the handful of articles that I had published and I rehearsed very professionally asking her for an assignment.

Well. When the time arrived, I started out just fine but I quickly devolved into begging, "Oh, please. Please. Just please let me write for you! I can. I know I can. I promise that I can!" This went on until Linda finally put a hand on my arm and told me to take a couple of deep breaths. So, I did. She then told me to take another one and, after I complied, she told me that she had agreed to give me an assignment at least one or two minutes before, but I hadn't heard her because I *wouldn't stop talking*.

Fortunately, Linda saw the humor in the situation and she instructed me to say: "What do you want me to write about? When do you need it? How much will you pay me?"

So, I did—and this was the start of a long and fruitful professional relationship. But, it raises the question of what else I've missed in life by not listening—and I'm not just referring to career-related moments. Who needed me to listen to their stories, whether it was joyful or something more poignant? Who needed me to pray for him or her, but I missed the opportunity? When should I just be still and listen?

One time, I visited someone in an assisted living facility with Reverend Smucker. I'd never met Gladys before, but her stories were fascinating as she shared how she'd served in World War II. Even her walls had stories to whisper, as they were adorned by a heartrending, beautiful piece of shattered silk, a gift from someone in Japan where the military she'd served with had fought so fiercely. My life would have been lessened had I not listened.

Writing exercise:

Is there someone at your church, at a local nursing home or elsewhere who would love for you to listen to his or her stories and record them for posterity? Could you help this person preserve memories for friends and family? What important stories will be lost if you don't? And, why not you? God surely gave you a love of words for a purpose.

Prayer:

God—I remember a teacher telling our elementary school class that we had two ears and only one mouth for a reason—so that we could spend more time listening and less time talking. Help me to give others time to share their stories, to not interrupt, to honor what they have to say. Help me to silence my lips when it's time and to speak healing words when it's time. Amen.

Week 47

So do not fear, for I am with you; do not be dismayed, for I am your God. I will strengthen you and help you; I will uphold you with my righteous right hand. (Isaiah 41:10)

One day, my newspaper editor asked me to interview a local photographer, Norbert, who volunteered his time to tape local school events for cable television. I called him and he was a pleasant man who was clearly making a difference in his community. But, I struggled to find the hook that's needed for a published article. As we were getting ready to hang up, though, I commented that he seemed to have a slight accent that disappeared as quickly as it arrived. That's all it took!

His story spilled out, with Norbert taking breaths only when necessary. He'd literally gone from millions to mayhem. He'd lived a pampered life in Hungary, as the only child of a wealthy doctor and his wife. They lived in a 24-room mansion filled with servants—plus a darkroom where young Norbert learned to develop film.

Then, Hitler invaded, and he and his parents ended up in a concentration camp where his mother died. American soldiers arrived on the day he and his father were released, with one of them realizing that Norbert was frightened; he gave the young boy his first piece of bubble gum. Norbert and his father immigrated to the United States, but the father's medical credentials weren't valid in their new homeland and he broke his back during manual labor. He spent the rest of his life in a nursing home. As for Norbert? He was a young man in a strange land, and he supported himself the only way he knew how. He took pictures.

I was stunned by this story and asked if I could share it with the newspaper's readers. His response? "This was a long time ago. You can share if you think someone would still be interested."

We don't know the power of our own stories, do we?

Writing exercise:

Evangelizing. Witnessing. Sharing the Good News. Those can sound like intimidating activities, for sure. But, one of the most powerful ways you can participate is by thinking about the times when God was clearly with you, when he strengthened you and helped you. Free write those stories, not worrying about what you'll share or won't share. Then, when you're done, is there someone who could benefit from hearing at least part of that story? Are you willing to share?

We've done similar exercises earlier in this year's devotionals. Is it getting easier to write your story? To share it with someone else?

Prayer:

God—you have created a unique life for me to live, which includes stories that only I can tell. Help me to recognize who needs to hear my story and give me the confidence to know that, if you want the story told, you will empower me to share, that you will uphold me with your righteous right hand. Amen.

Week 48

For everything God created is good, and nothing is to be rejected if it is received with thanksgiving. (I Timothy 4:4)

Praise him, all his angels; praise him, all his heavenly hosts. Praise him, sun and moon; praise him, all you shining stars. Praise him, you highest heavens and you waters above the skies. Let them praise the name of the Lord, for at his command they were created, (Psalm 148:2-5)

Our church has recently undergone an in-depth search for a new pastor. The woman who was facilitating the search explained that, in Presbyterian tradition, we believe that God is really doing the work of matching a church with its new pastor. Meanwhile, our job was to be in prayer and to listen for and be receptive to God's presence and direction.

As she was explaining this belief, I started to imagine a rolodex. *God's rolodex!*

Now, as you already know, God is the creator of the universe. Having formed us in his image, he has gifted us with creative energy (read: imaginations!) and I believe that he delights in us whenever we use that God-given gift in life-affirming ways.

(I also believe that God sympathizes with the grownups who spend time with children with active imaginations. When my grandparents would drop me off after I'd stayed with them, my grandfather would inevitably say something like, "Kelly . . . well . . . things went great . . . but . . . she has TOO much imagination." Do you have similar stories?)

With that caveat in place, let me share that I imagine God's rolodex to be humongous, with each of us having a card containing our name. Each card would contain heavenly hyperlinks cross referencing the various ways in which God plans to use us in his service—and, perhaps when he touches a link, lightning flashes and thunder booms! Maybe he even calls over a guardian angel or two to reminisce: "Boy, THAT was a close one. Do you remember that day?"

Obviously, God doesn't NEED to reference a rolodex card, ever. He intimately knows each one of us—and did so, even before we were born. As Luke 12:7 assures us, "Indeed, the very hairs of your head are all numbered." I nevertheless imagine that God enjoys flipping through the rolodex cards, much as we might huddle up with a photo album containing pictures of our loved ones.

What do you think?

Writing exercise:

Imagine that God allows you a glimpse at your rolodex card. What does the card contain that might surprise you? Let your imagination fly as you free write the astonishing plans that God has for you. Let's say that the card also contains names of people that he intends to be in your life. Who is on the list that you need to get back in touch with? Make amends with?

Prayer:

God—it is such a blessing to rest in the sure and certain knowledge that you intimately know and care for me. You have an entire universe at your fingertips and, yet, you have taken the time to craft a unique plan for my life. Help me to have the courage to take the steps that I have feared to take and forgive me for any resistance. God's will, not my will, be done! Amen.

Week 49

The Lord reigneth; let the earth rejoice; let the multitude of isles be glad thereof. (Psalm 97:1, King James Version)

The first three words of Psalm 97 appear on the Memorial Arch, located in the town square of Oberlin, Ohio. This memorial honors the Oberlin Band, Christian missionaries from Oberlin College who traveled to the Shanxi province of China in the 1880s. They were, unfortunately, ill prepared for their work, unable to even speak the language. Then, rumors apparently spread that the missionaries were poisoning water in the wells. In response, fifteen of the missionaries— men, women and children—were executed by the government or killed during the Boxer Rebellion in the summer of 1900.

If you approach the Memorial Arch from the park side, you'll see this phrase: "The Lord Reigneth." If you approach the monument from the street side, though, you'll see these words "Ye Are Witnesses," most likely a reference to Isaiah 43:10: "Ye are my witnesses, saith the Lord, and my servant whom I have chosen: that ye may know and believe me, and understand that I am he: before me there was no God formed, neither shall there be after me."

Whenever I visit this monument, I stop to read the names of the people who were martyred, to be a witness to happened to them. For some reason, one name always jumps out at me: Ernestine Harriet Atwater, killed on July 9, 1900. I wonder what people called her. Did people close to her affectionately call her Tina? Hat, as a shortened version of Harriet? Or maybe she preferred her entire regal name spoken aloud: *Ernestine Harriet.* I just don't know.

One of the greatest privileges as a writer, I believe, is the opportunity to be the voice of someone whose actual voice was silenced, as hers was—or to be the voice of someone whose name was never even considered important enough to be recorded on a monument. Perhaps the voice of a slave who escaped to Oberlin or that of a frightened woman who found the courage to guide that slave along the Underground Railroad route.

The voiceless person who speaks to me may not, of course, be the same one who speaks to you. This person may belong to ages past or might be struggling to make ends meet today. What is certain: someone needs you to speak up for him or her. To paraphrase Martin Luther King, our lives begin to end when we stop speaking out about what matters. *What person needs you?*

Writing exercise:

Choose someone from the past who intrigues you. You may know this person's name—like I know the name of Ernestine Harriet Atwater—or you may only know this person as one of a multitude who got caught up in a horrific situation. Write a letter for that person. Consider doing research so that you can more accurately speak up for that voiceless person.

Now look in today's news stories. Who needs you to speak up NOW, perhaps through a letter to the editor or by writing an article drawing attention to a plight—or perhaps by requesting help for that person through your church's mission programs?

Prayer:

God—it is so easy to remain silent, caught up in busywork of the day. Help me to slow down and take notice of those who are helpless, voiceless, and who need someone of faith to speak up for them. Give me the words to speak, guide my hands and feet. Amen.

Week 50

What good is it, my brothers and sisters, if someone claims to have faith but has no deeds? Can such faith save them? Suppose a brother or a sister is without clothes and daily food. If one of you says to them, "Go in peace; keep warm and well fed," but does nothing about their physical needs, what good is it? In the same way, faith by itself, if it is not accompanied by action, is dead. (James 2:14-17)

Isaac Monah had a difficult childhood. He lived in Liberia and, in 1989, his home was destroyed in a bloody war. His younger brother? Killed. Isaac fled to the Ivory Coast and then to Ghana, where he finally earned a high school diploma at the age of 27.

While in the Ivory Coast, he helped an American anthropology student track monkeys in the jungle and they discussed their faith, with the student using a word that Isaac hadn't heard before: Presbyterian.

When Isaac immigrated to the United States, he settled in Ohio and began working as a nurse's aide—and attending a church that had that word on their sign: Presbyterian. He couldn't forget his homeland, though, where 82% of the population was living in grueling poverty. So, he and his pastor traveled to Liberia, where Isaac felt a calling to give children there something he had longed for as a child: an education.

His church was enthusiastic about the project, but had no money to give him. Nevertheless, their support kept his dream alive, and then the parents of a brain cancer patient that Isaac was caring for persuaded their church to help fund a school in the Twarbo region of Liberia where—ready for this—no school existed. Not one.

Momentum began to build, with other churches joining in. Then, a former pastor of Isaac's—who was now working for the United

Nations—wrote a letter of support. On November 30, 2012, the school opened, supported by four schools and thirty worship communities.

A German hunger and poverty aid group dug a well for the school and is repairing bridges. Another international health care organization is helping the school with transportation and communication challenges, and even Ebola couldn't stop the momentum. Although all Liberian schools closed for seven months during the epidemic, Isaac's school—the Dougbe River Presbyterian School—reopened in 2015 with 152 students.

Isaac clearly spearheaded this project and deserves enormous credit. But, it took the enthusiasm of his pastor, the support of his church, and the participation of other churches and schools and health care organizations to make this happen. And, what about the student who, in the darkness of the Ivory Coast jungle, witnessed for Jesus Christ?

How can you be a link in the chain that makes the impossible . . . possible?

Writing exercise:

Isaac was an important link in the chain, a crucial cog in the wheel. Consider sketching out a chain or a wheel—or some other meaningful image—and then find examples in your life where you can make connections that are needed to make a difference in the lives of others. What would your chain look like?

Prayer:

God—we lift up the Dougbe River Presbyterian School in our prayers today. May the children, teachers, parents and community flourish. We pray for mission coworkers around the world who take significant risks with their own health, safety and wellbeing to care for others and to share Christian love in practical, meaningful ways. Give me courage to do my part, whatever you have planned for me. Amen.

Week 51

Create in me a pure heart, O God, and renew a steadfast spirit within me. Do not cast me from your presence or take your Holy Spirit from me. Restore to me the joy of your salvation and grant me a willing spirit, to sustain me. Then I will teach transgressors your ways, so that sinners will turn back to you. Deliver me from the guilt of bloodshed, O God, you who are God my Savior, and my tongue will sing of your righteousness. Open my lips, Lord, and my mouth will declare your praise. (Psalm 51: 10-15)

But the father said to his servants, 'Quick! Bring the best robe and put it on him. Put a ring on his finger and sandals on his feet. Bring the fattened calf and kill it. Let's have a feast and celebrate. For this son of mine was dead and is alive again; he was lost and is found.' So they began to celebrate. (Luke 15:22-24)

If you have participated in all of these devotional exercises—or even some of them—you have, in effect, been writing your spiritual autobiography. As an imperfect human, you've probably faced less than wonderful parts of yourself, and that can feel discouraging. That's understandable.

But, let's go back to the beginning of this book: to the foreword where King David was described as a man who used the arts as a form of worship. This includes the writing of many psalms—and the one being quoted for this devotional was written after David was caught in an adulterous affair with Bathsheba. Not only did David have an affair; after he discovered that Bathsheba was expecting his baby, he sent her husband Uriah to the frontlines of a fierce battle where he was killed.

As the Reverend Marek P. Zabriskie points out in *The Bible Challenge*, David broke the fifth, sixth, seventh, eighth, ninth and tenth commandments all in one fell swoop. That's significant sin! And yet, he came to God with a contrite heart and was ultimately forgiven. He didn't make excuses. He didn't try to blame someone else. He didn't claim kingly privileges.

He simply admitted his fault, was repentant and confessed his need for God's forgiveness.

Then there is the parable of the prodigal son, found in Luke. The younger son had taken his share of his father's wealth and squandered it on wild living. When he came home, he hoped to work as a hired hand, not expecting anything more. Yet, you see his father's response: *This son of mine was dead and is alive again; he was lost and is found.*

Is there something in your life that is preventing you from returning home to God? Do you feel as though you've done something unforgiveable? Are you filled with shame? If so, then meditate on these two Bible passages and embrace the incredible grace of God, who is simply saying: Come home, child. Just come home.

Writing exercise:

Write down your feelings in response to these two passages. Then, read them aloud to God.

God is faithful. He is just. He will forgive us our sins and purify us from all unrighteousness. Praise God!

Prayer:

God—your grace is so overwhelming that I struggle to take it all in. You, the creator of the universe, care this much for me! Help me to root out any unconfessed sin that separates me from you. Help me to confess, even when it's scary, and transform me so that I can honor you with my thoughts, words and deeds. Amen.

Week 52

Guide me in your truth and teach me, for you are God my Savior, and my hope is in you all day long. (Psalm 25:5)

Any spiritual journey is, if authentically embraced, a journey towards truth. Significant truths often come to us in pieces, rather than all at once—and that is what is happening with me when I consider a question recently posed.

When on the mini-pilgrimage at the Order of the Sisters of St. Francis, our group paused in front of a statue of St. Francis with a wild wolf that he was said to have tamed. The question that we were asked to consider was: *I think the untamed wolf in me is _____. How do I address it?*

I found that question intriguing and have tried to answer. But, I can't. At least not yet. When you find that happening on your spiritual journey, you may need to approach a question sideways, knowing that you're only chipping away at the surface of the answer. One way to do this is to write about yourself as if you were part of a myth or legend. I tried that technique with the wolf question and here is draft one. If I try this exercise again in a year, my guess is that I will have gotten closer to the wolf. But, for now:

On a mountain, there lived a wolf. He was sleek and sharp fanged, and the mountain was steep and jagged, covered by a thick and humid mist. A woman also lived on the mountain. Each day she gathered plants and collected water from the river for her needs, staying close to what was familiar and safe. She knew that something beautiful existed on the other side of the mountain but, even though she had never seen the wolf, she knew of him—and she knew that the wolf was blocking her path.

If she got too close to him, she could sense him by smell and her chest tightened in fear, so she would scurry back to the safety of her cave. Finally, though, she decided that enough was enough. She was going to confront that wolf!

She then tried her hardest to get close to him, but never could. Sometimes, terror overtook her and she fled. Other times, she felt strong—but the sly and slippery wolf could not be found. No matter what her plan, it did not work. Finally she cried out to God for help.

God agreed to help her with the wolf and she eagerly awaited the fulfillment of that promise. But, instead of taking her nearer to the wolf, he took her along long and winding paths, where she often stumbled, sometimes fell—and even got injured.

The woman finally called out in frustration, "God, you promised to guide me to the wolf, to where I could finally deal with him once and for all. Why haven't you done as you promised?"

"I've done exactly what I promised," he told her.

"I'm no better off than before—and, in many ways, worse!" she cried. "So, if you didn't plan to help me to actually defeat the wolf, why didn't you at least take my hand and walk me around the wolf? Then, I could have gotten to the other side without harm!"

He was silent for a moment and the woman feared that she had gone too far, that she had angered God. But, when he finally spoke, his words and tone were gentle. "My daughter," he said, "you have been circling that same wolf your entire life. If I simply retraced your journey, it would only have made you wearier."

The woman was outraged. "You haven't been taking me on a path at all! We've just been winding around the mountain for days, months—and even years—in meaningless ways."

"Not so random," God countered. "This journey has made your stronger, has it not?"

"Well, yes."

"That strength will help you when you finally meet the wolf," God promised. "And, after you nearly slipped off the cliff, you learned how to plant your feet more firmly. So this journey has made you wiser, has it not?"

"Well . . . yes."

"And, when we first began, you hesitated to hold my hand, even when I encircled yours. Now, you sometimes reach out for mine! Is this journey therefore not making you more faithful?"

"Yes," the woman replied, "but it's all been so hard! If you are all powerful, and if it didn't make sense to circle the wolf, then why didn't you just defang the beast?"

Again, she feared God's wrath. But, instead, she sensed a gentle smile. "If I did that," he said, "I would just be giving you another way to avoid the wolf. Instead, he needs tamed."

"Tamed? How on earth can I tame this wolf when I can't even get near his ferocious teeth?"

"Take a look at your journey, thus far," God said. "You trust me more now, despite your winding path. Before, you didn't even talk to me—and now you feel close enough to me to question me! And, the more that you trust in me, the more I'm giving you the gift of trusting yourself. As this grows, you will get closer."

"And then?"

"Then," God responded, "you will get close enough to realize that you are the wolf and the wolf is you. When you can fully embrace that truth, you will have harnessed the wildness of the wolf and can use his spirit to fulfill the purpose I had for you, even before you were born."

Writing exercise:

What myth or legend can you write about your own life? You can use the question posed by the Sisters or go in another direction. What truths is your story pointing you towards?

Prayer:

God—there are stories in my life that are still too challenging for me to face, head on. Help me to turn those over to you, knowing that healing and wholeness come through you and that you can use all for good. Take what is hurting in me, God, and use it for your glory.

Amen.

Appendix I

If you'd like to publish your devotionals, the overall process is to:

1) Search for potential markets.
2) Read their writer's guidelines.
3) Decide if a publication is a good fit for your work.
4) If so, create a devotional(s) for that market.
5) Submit appropriately, according to guidelines.
6) If you find success, continue to submit to that market.
7) If you don't find success but still think you're a good fit with a market, try a few more times.
8) Continue to search for markets. You can add a new twist to previous devotionals or write brand new ones.

One dozen leads: find appropriate markets for devotionals

1) Read relevant sections of the current year of Writer's Market: http://www.writersmarket.com/
2) Read relevant sections of the current year of Christian Writer's Market Guide: http://stuartmarket.com/
3) Alive Now: http://alivenow.upperroom.org/writers/
4) The Upper Room: http://devotional.upperroom.org/guidelines
5) Augsburg Fortress: http://www.augsburgfortress.org/company/submit.jsp
6) Forward Movement: http://www.forwardmovement.org/Pages/About/Writers_Guidelines.aspx
7) Judson Press: http://www.judsonpress.com/catalog_sp_guidelines.cfm
8) Standard Publishing: http://store.standardpub.com/Pages/About/For_Writers.aspx

9) These Days:
   http://www.pahsa.org/uploads/writing-guidelines-for-these-days-.pdf
10) Devozine (for teens):
   http://devozine.upperroom.org/write-for-us/writers-guidelines/
11) The Wesleyan Church: https://www.wesleyan.org/wg
12) Thriving Family: http://www.thrivingfamily.com/extra/call-for-submissions

Appendix II: Further Reading

Cepero, Helen, *Journaling as a Spiritual Practice: Encountering God Through Attentive Writing* (IVP Books, 2008)

Desalvo, Louise, *Writing as a Way of Healing: How Telling Our Stories Transforms Our Lives* (Beacon Press, 2000)

Gray, Bonnie, *Finding Spiritual Whitespace: Awakening Your Soul to Rest* (Revell, 2014)

Handler, Jessica, *Braving the Fire: A Guide to Writing About Grief and Loss* (St. Martin's Griffin, 2013)

Hering, Karen, *Writing to Wake the Soul: Opening the Sacred Conversation Within* (Atria Books/Beyond Words, 2013)

Hoover, Sharon Recher, *Soul Motive to Pray: A Personal Retreat Paperback* (CreateSpace Independent Publishing Platform, 2013)

Norris, Kathleen, *The Cloister Walk* (Riverhead Books, 1997)

Schneider, Pat, *How the Light Gets In: Writing as a Spiritual Practice* (Oxford University Press, 2013)

Vecchione, Patrice, *Writing and the Spiritual Life: Finding Your Voice by Looking Within* (McGraw-Hill; 1 edition (April 21, 2001)

Vincent, Kristen E., *A Bead and a Prayer: A Beginner's Guide to Protestant Prayer Beads* (Upper Room, 2013)

Zinsser, William, *Going on Faith: Writing As a Spiritual Quest Paperback* (De Capo Press, 1999)

CPSIA information can be obtained
at www.ICGtesting.com
Printed in the USA
FFOW02n1257171215
19425FF